Iraq

Iraq

BY
LEILA MERRELL FOSTER

Enchantment of the World
Second Series

Children's Press®

A Division of Grolier Publishing

NEW YORK   LONDON   HONG KONG   SYDNEY
DANBURY, CONNECTICUT

Consultant: Louay Bahry, Ph.D., Adjunct Professor of Political Science, University of Tennessee, Knoxville

Please note: All statistics are as up-to-date as possible at the time of publication.

Visit Children's Press on the Internet at: http://publishing.grolier.com

Library of Congress Cataloging-in-Publication Data

Foster, Leila Merrell.
      Iraq / by Leila Merrell Foster.
      p. cm. — (Enchantment of the world. Second series)
      Includes bibliographical references (p.   ) and index.
Summary: Describes the history, geography, history, culture, industry, and people of
      Iraq, formerly known as Mesopotamia.
      ISBN 0-516-20584-6
      1. Iraq—Juvenile literature. [1. Iraq.] I. Title. II. Series
      DS70.6.F67 1997
      956.7—dc21   97-2005
                                                    CIP
                                                     AC

To Leila Virginia Merrell Foster and
George Henry Foster,
my mother and father, who gave me a love for travel
and a curiosity about other countries

Cover photo:
Askari Shrine

Contents

CHAPTER

The northeastern foothills

Saddam Hussein

The Koran

CHAPTER ONE

An Ancient Civilization

People who lived long ago in the land that is now Iraq have given us so much. The book you are reading now owes a great deal to an ancient system of writing developed by these people. They may also have been the first ones to grasp mathematical ideas, such as two plus two equals four.

W HEN YOU GET INTO A CAR, PERHAPS you should thank these people who started using the wheel in transportation five thousand years ago. Look at the clock, and think of these people who decided to have sixty minutes in an hour. Curious about the universe, they reported seeing a supernova star some six thousand years ago. Inventive, too, they developed a system of irrigation for their crops, and they were among the first people to live together in cities.

Then these people developed strong empires. They built forts and palaces. They even designed a hanging garden that was one of the wonders of the ancient world. At one time, their capital city was the center of learning for the whole world.

Today, Iraq is a nation with enormous economic potential. Its oil resources are among the largest in the world. Its

Some areas of Iraq are beautiful, and the people are wealthy.

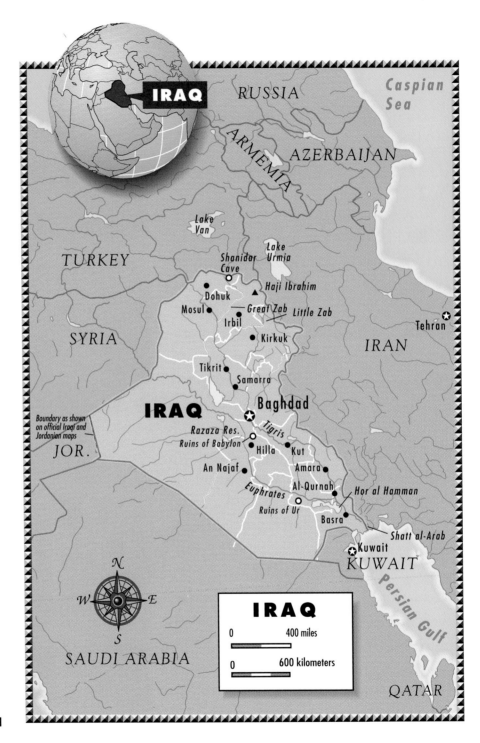

Geopolitical map of Iraq

population and water supply are large enough to develop other industries in its economy. Yet, in recent years, the actions of Saddam Hussein have burdened the Iraqis with debt and deprived them of food.

Strategically located at the eastern edge of the Arab countries, Iraq is a barrier to the expansion of its neighbor to the east—Iran. Saudi Arabia and Kuwait to the south have great oil resources that are needed in the industries of many countries, ranging from the United States and Canada to Europe and Japan. If Iraq or the former Soviet Union to the north controlled all the Middle East oil, the world's industrial nations would be in serious trouble.

With all Iraq's resources of oil, water, and labor plus the political assets in its location, how did Iraq of today plunge into so much misfortune? The current ruler, Saddam Hussein, put down other groups who wanted to share power. Like some rulers before him, he murdered Iraqis who dared to oppose him—or anyone he thought might try to overthrow him. For eight years, Iraq fought a war with Iran during which a large number of

In other areas, people are poor.

Iraqis were killed or wounded. By invading Kuwait, a neighboring country Hussein claimed as Iraqi territory, Hussein brought the full force of United Nations (U.N.) economic sanctions and multinational armies against him and his country.

Saddam Hussein ordered the invasion of Kuwait, claiming it as Iraqi territory.

CHAPTER

TWO

The Land Between Two Rivers

The territory of Iraq is where much of civilization began. Many great empires built their capitals here and extended their power throughout the Fertile Crescent and beyond. The Fertile Crescent is the territory that is roughly shaped like a crescent and follows the population settlements between the Tigris and Euphrates rivers from the Mediterranean Sea to the Persian Gulf. For centuries, important trade routes between the Eastern and Western worlds crossed this area.

Beautiful cliffs are part of Iraq's geography.

THE ANCIENT NAME FOR THE TERritory of Iraq is Mesopotamia, which means "the Land Between Two Rivers"—the Tigris and the Euphrates. Its modern name, Iraq, is the Arabic word for cliff—a geographic feature of the country.

Iraq is a little larger than the U.S. state of California or the South American country of Paraguay. Its area is 167,925 square miles (434,925 sq km).

Boundaries

Some of Iraq's boundaries are relatively new. On the east, Iraq shares a boundary with Iran; on the north, with Turkey; on the northwest with Syria; on the southwest, with Jordan and Saudi Arabia; on the south, with Saudi Arabia, Kuwait, and the waters of the Persian Gulf.

As recently as 1926, the northern province, including the city of Mosul and rich oil deposits, became part of Iraq, though Turkey claimed the area. Also in the north are people called Kurds, who hope to have their own nation. Boundary disputes with Iran were one of the reasons for the war of 1980 to 1988 with that country.

Geographical features

Area: 167,925 square miles (434,925 sq km)

Average Summer Temperature: (May to October) 70°F to 110°F (20°C to 43°C)

Average Winter Temperature: (December to March) 50°F (10°C)

Average Annual Rainfall: 4 to 7 inches (10 to 18 cm)

Major Rivers: The Tigris River stretches for 1,150 miles (1,851 km) and the Euphrates for 1,460 miles (2,350 km). Both begin in the highlands of Turkey. The Euphrates moves through Syria. Finally they converge into the Shatt al-Arab, which flows for 115 miles (185 km) before spilling into the Persian Gulf.

Boundary lengths:

Turkey, 190 miles (306 km)

Iran, 906 miles (1,458 km)

Kuwait, 158 miles (254 km)

Saudi Arabia, 556 miles (895 km)

Jordan, 91 miles (147 km)

Syria, 375 miles (604 km)

Persian Gulf Coastline, 12 miles (19 km)

Territorial Sea Limit: 12 miles (19 km)

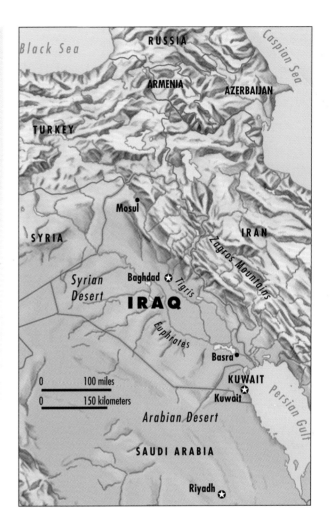

Topographical map of Iraq

Geographical Zones

Iraq has four main geographical divisions: desert in the west and southwest, dry rolling grasslands between the upper Tigris and Euphrates Rivers, highlands in the north and east, and a plain through which the lower Tigris and Euphrates flow.

The desert that stretches west and south of the Euphrates River is part of a larger desert area that extends into Syria,

The Land Between Two Rivers **15**

The Iraqi desert

Jordan, and Saudi Arabia. Few people live on this stony plain that is lined with wadis—streams that are dry most of the year. During the winter season, however, rain sends dangerous flash floods down these wadis.

The rolling upland area, between the Tigris River north of Samarra and the Euphrates north of Hit, is sometimes called al-Jazirah (the island). The water here has cut deep valleys that make irrigation difficult, but there is some rain-fed agriculture.

The highlands have mountainous areas.

The highlands begin just southwest of the cities of Mosul and Kirkuk and extend to the borders with Iran. The foothills and plains meet mountains ranging from 3,000 to 12,000 feet (914 to 3,658 m) near the borders of Iran and Turkey. The mountain area has several valleys suitable for agriculture. However, in the foothills and plains, the soil and rainfall can support crops. Great oil fields are found near Kirkuk, the center of the region.

The low plain of Baghdad begins north of the city, Iraq's capital, and extends to the Persian Gulf. Most of Iraq's people live in or near this plain.

The plain is called alluvial because it is built up by mud and sediment laid down by rivers. In many places, the Tigris and Euphrates Rivers are above the level of the plain—like the Mississippi River in the southern United States.

This 45,000-square-mile (116,550-sq-km) area is the delta, the point where rivers flow into the gulf—an area grooved by river channels and irrigation canals. When the rivers flood, temporary lakes form. The silt carried by the river, the irrigation canals, and the wind build up the delta plains at the rate of about 8 inches (20 cm) a century. Heavy flooding can result in deposits of up to 12 inches (30

The lowlands are covered in water in many spots.

Farming is difficult in the high-water areas.

The Land Between Two Rivers **17**

Iraq's Major Cities

Basra (above) is situated on the Shatt al-Arab River, 340 miles (550 km) southeast of Baghdad and 80 miles (130 km) from the Persian Gulf. It is Iraq's chief seaport and second largest city. Omar Caliph, a religious and political leader, founded the city in A.D. 637, and it quickly became the focal point of Arab sea trade.

Mosul is located 246 miles (396 km) north of Baghdad in Iraq's northern highlands. It is one of the largest cities in Iraq and the most ethnically diverse, populated by Arabs, Kurds, Assyrians, and Turkomans. Traditionally, cotton was the most important export from this city and the word muslin is derived from Mosul. The rich oil fields surrounding Mosul, however, became the main source of revenue in the area.

Irbil, located 52 miles (84 km) east of Mosul in north Iraq, is the headquarters of the Kurdish Autonomous Region. As the center of Kurdish resistance to Saddam Hussein's rule, it has several times been the source of violent clashes between government and Kurdish troops and between rival Kurdish factions. Irbil is one of the oldest continuously inhabited cities in the world—Neolithic people roamed the area some 10,000 years ago.

For information on Iraq's capital city, Baghdad, see the sidebar in Chapter Five.

cm) of mud in some of the temporary lakes. Unfortunately, the rivers also carry large quantities of salts that damage crops. Because of the high water table and poor drainage, these salts concentrate near the surface. As a result, farming in the region south of al-Amarah is limited.

A large part of this area was once a marshland that extended into Iran. After the Gulf War, perhaps to destroy rebel bases hidden in this marshland, Saddam Hussein built a canal to drain the marshes and divert the water to desert land. Many of the area's people, known as the Marsh Arabs, had to flee across the border to Iran.

Iraq's Major Lakes

Tharthar Lake
Razzaza Lake
Habbaniyah Lake

Dhows on the Shatt al-Arab

The Rivers

The two great rivers of Iraq are the Tigris and the Euphrates. The waters of these rivers are an important resource of the country and undoubtedly made the beginning of civilization possible here. People were able to settle in cities and could plant food and move about by boat.

The Tigris begins in Turkey and flows into Iraq. The Euphrates also begins in Turkey, then flows into Syria, and on into Iraq. The Tigris and the Euphrates meet in southern Iraq at al-Qurnah to form the river known as the Shatt al-Arab, which flows into the Persian Gulf. The Shatt al-Arab is the waterway involved in the disputed boundary with Iran.

The Tigris River at the center of Baghdad

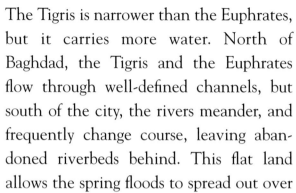

The rivers serve as a water highway.

The Tigris is narrower than the Euphrates, but it carries more water. North of Baghdad, the Tigris and the Euphrates flow through well-defined channels, but south of the city, the rivers meander, and frequently change course, leaving abandoned riverbeds behind. This flat land allows the spring floods to spread out over a large area. Also, because the Tigris can rise at the rate of 12 inches (30 cm) per hour, flash floods may occur. Flood control and irrigation systems now help to prevent some of the destruction experienced in the past.

Through the centuries, the rivers have been used as water highways. Yet, they also create problems for modern transportation. Flooding in the lower sections makes road-building difficult. The fast current in the upper regions of the rivers prevents boats from traveling upstream. Near the gulf, the rivers are wide and slow, but often very shallow. Dredging is necessary to allow shipping in these waters.

Climate

Iraq has two seasons: winter (the wet season) and summer (the dry season). During the six months from November through April, the country gets 90 percent of its annual rainfall. Most of the rain comes during the winter, from December to March. The dry season lasts from May to October. June, July, and August are very hot months.

The mean, or average, annual rainfall is between 4 and 7 inches (10 and 18 cm) except in the mountains of the north and northeast, where rain is more plentiful. Some spots there receive 40 inches (102 cm) a year. Because of the rugged terrain, however, the rain is not useful for cultivation of crops. In the valleys, foothills, and plains, where 12 inches (30 cm) or more of rain fall each year, agriculture is possible without irrigation. But even here, a shortage of rain can lead to crop failure and only one crop a year can be grown.

In desert areas, rain can be a problem as well as a gift. Five or six days of steady rain can turn roads into thick mud and disrupt mail and telephone service. Planted crops are often washed out. Houses and roofs made of mud can leak badly. Fortunately, most buildings can be repaired when the rain stops.

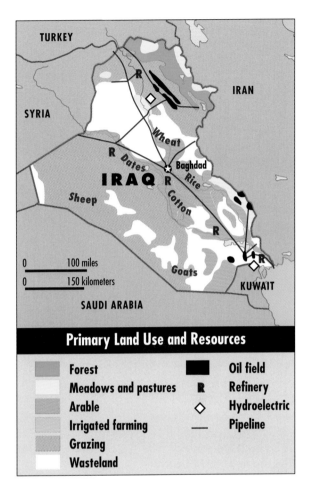

Primary Land Use and Resources

Forest
Meadows and pastures
Arable
Irrigated farming
Grazing
Wasteland
Oil field
R Refinery
◇ Hydroelectric
— Pipeline

In some areas, winter weather can be quite harsh.

Most Iraqis enjoy the market after 6:00 P.M., when the temperatures are cooler.

Winter temperatures may reach below freezing in the north and northeastern foothills and the western deserts. Summer temperatures range from 70° F to 110° F (20° C to 43° C). Extreme temperatures in the western desert go from 6° F to more than 115° F (-14° C to 46° C).

Around the rivers and irrigation canals, humidity adds to the discomfort. The city of Baghdad comes alive in the summer after 6 P.M. when it is cool enough to enjoy the markets, the parks, and the restaurants. In the country, a cool summer night is also a time

A dust storm covering an Iraqi hotel

for activity and visiting. The heat of the day is good only for sleeping and saving one's energy.

Two types of wind are famous in Iraq. A dry wind from the south called a sharqi can gust up to 50 miles (80 km) an hour. It carries dust that rises so high in the air that it often closes down airports. These storms usually come at the change of the seasons. In mid-June to mid-September, the prevailing wind from the north and northwest is called the shamal. The very dry air of the shamal permits the sun to heat up the land, though the breeze does help to cool it a little.

The shortage of rain and the extreme heat make much of Iraq a desert. Soil and plants lose any moisture they get from the rain very quickly through evaporation.

Agriculture's Beginnings

Suppose you lived 14,000 years ago. When you felt hungry, you could not go out to a restaurant. You could not even go to a farm to get supplies. You and your family would live apart from others because you needed space to hunt animals and gather seeds and plants. Your days would be spent hunting and gathering to get food, clothing, and shelter.

NOW IMAGINE YOURSELF LIVING 12,000 YEARS AGO. About that time, you heard of a new way to get food. Now you gathered seeds and planted them. You caught wild animals and tamed them. You were the first farmers with crops and herds of animals. You could settle down in one place instead of moving about searching for food.

Archaeologists—scientists who study ancient people— think that Iraq is one of the first places where farming began. In northern Iraq, wild barley and wheat grew, and wild sheep and goats roamed. To learn how ancient people lived, scientists now study seeds and bones as well as the tools they find.

Humans had been around for thousands of years before the first evidence of agriculture, so why did it take so long to come up with this idea? As far as climate was concerned, it should have been possible to farm before then. But they needed tools to capture animals and grind grain. And they needed social skills, such as language, to tell each other about important discoveries.

Even after they learned about farming, though, people had to decide whether it was worth the extra work. Agriculture took a lot more time and effort than hunting and gathering. What were its advantages? The people had more control of

their food supply. Mothers could settle down in one place, so it was safer to raise children. Animals could provide milk and wool. And some people could work at other jobs—making pottery, building houses, and teaching.

Animals and When They Were Domesticated

Goat	About 8500 B.C.
Sheep	About 8000 B.C.
Pig	About 7500 B.C.
Cattle and Cat	About 7000 B.C.
Donkey and Horse	About 4000 B.C.
Camel	About 3000 B.C.

The horse and the camel were domesticated so late because these animals disappeared during the Ice Age and were late in reappearing in this area.

Master of the Animals

When you look at the sculptures left by ancient people, you can see that humans did not always win in a contest with animals. Sometimes, the lion is standing over the man, and it's the lion who's going to have dinner. It is not surprising then that a hero was often portrayed as the "master of the animals."

This winged figure sits at the entrance to a temple.

Gazelles are native to Iraq.

Our domestic animals were not all tamed at the same time. The first was probably the wolf which was tamed to become a dog and help with hunting. That may have happened about 13,000 years ago.

Because of the power animals had, the gods worshiped by these early people sometimes had a crown of horns, wings, an animal head, or a cloak of fish. Huge statues of winged bulls with human heads stood in their palaces as symbols of the ruler's power.

Of course, Iraq still has wild animals, though they are not the problem they were in ancient times when there were more of them. In some

Ships of the Desert

Camels, sometimes called ships of the desert, provide a means of travel in a desert. They can go without water for long periods. They eat spiny desert plants. Their big feet help them walk easily on sand. Their eyes and nostrils close up for protection against blowing sand. Camels also provide milk and flesh for food, and hair for clothing and tents. However, they are stubborn animals who express themselves by kicking and spitting. It is small wonder that in a land with cheap oil, the four-wheel-drive truck is more popular than the camel today.

locations, you still might find gazelles, wild asses, hyenas, wolves, foxes, jackals, wild pigs, hares, jerboas (a rodent), and bats. Then there are tortoises, snakes, lizards, and frogs as well as fish and shellfish. Many birds of prey such as vultures and hawks also live in the region. Ducks, geese, and partridges provide food for the people in the area. Falcons are trained for hunting.

Plants

Not much vegetation exists in Iraq. However, dates of the date palm are exported. A date palm begins to bear fruit by the eighth year, is mature at thirty, and begins to decline around one hundred.

Willow, poplar, and alder trees are found in the south. In the mountains to the north, the valonia oak is grown for its bark, used in tanning leather. The barley and wheat that helped to start the agricultural revolution are still important and much improved over the ancient crop, thanks to selective planting.

Date palm

Opposite: **Hawks inhabit some regions.**

World Empires

Many important civilizations bloomed in Iraq. Sumerians, Akkadians, Babylonians, Assyrians, Persians, Greeks, Romans, Arabs, Mongols, and Turks have all called this country home and contributed to modern Iraq. The history of humans can be traced far back in time to discover how people lived in these great civilizations.

E

Before Written History

VEN WITHOUT WRITTEN RECORDS, ARCHAE-ologists are able to tell us how people lived by examining what they left behind. Hand axes and scrapers dating back to 120,000 B.C. have been found in northern Iraq. Some of these artifacts were found at ancient campsites or workshops; others were found in caves.

In the Shanidar Cave, scientists found the skull of a Neanderthal man (a prehistoric human being). Some skeletons found higher in the cave may date back to about 45,000 years ago. Those found at the lower levels may be 60,000 years old.

The skull of a Neanderthal

About 9,000 years ago, great changes took place in northern Iraq and surrounding areas. Humans settled in one place and built houses out of clay, which was plentiful. They began to use metal in place of the limited supply of stone. Several families lived together and figured out how to govern themselves. Villages grew to be cities. Over time, cities formed kingdoms and eventually the kingdoms became empires.

This wax reconstruction shows what a Neanderthal man might have looked like.

World Empires **31**

Timeline of rulers of Iraq (both ancient and modern)

The Kingdom of Assyria	B.C.		B.C.
		King Shamshi-Adad V	824–812
King Ashur-nadir-ahe	1410–1393	King Adadnirari III	811–783
King Enib-Adad	1392–1381	King Shalmaneser IV	782–773
King Ahur-yuballidh	1380–1341	King Ashur-dan III	772–764
King Enlil-nirari	1340–1326	King Hadad-nirari IV	763–755
King Arik-den-ili	1325–1311	King Ashur-nirari V	754–747
King Adadnirari I	1310–1281	King Tiglath-pileser III	746–728
King Shalmaneser I	1280–1261	King Shalmaneser V	727–722
King Tululti-Ninurta I	1260–1232	King Sargon II	722–705
King Ashur nasir pal I	1231–1214	King Sennacherib	705–682
King Ashur-nirari III	1213–1208	King Esarhaddon	681–669
King Bel-Kudur-uzur	1207–1203	King Ashurbanipal	669–630
King Ninurta-apal-ekur I	1202–1176	King Ashur-etil-ilani	630–627
King Mutakkil-Nusku	1175–1141	King Sin-shar-iskun	627–612
King Ashur-res-isi	1140–1138		
King Tiglath-pileser I	1115–1103	**The Kingdom of Babylon**	**B.C.**
King Ninurta-apal-ekur II	1102–1093	King Sumuabi	2049–2036
King Ashur-bel-kala I	1092–1076	King Sumu-lailu	2035–2000
King Enlil-rabi	1075–1069	King Sin-muballit	1812–1793
King Enriba-Adad	1061–1056	King Hammurabi	1792–1750
King Shamshi-Adad IV	1055–1050	King Samsu-iluna	1750–1712
King Ashurnasirpal I	1049–1031	King Abeshuh	1712–1684
King Shalmaneser II	1030–1019	King Ammi-ditana	1684–1647
King Ashur-nirari IV	1018–1013	King Ammi-zaduga	1647–1626
King Ashur-rabi II	1012–995	King Samsuditana	1626–1595
King Ashur-res-isi II	994–967	**(Unknown dynasty)**	
King Tiglath-pileser II	956–934	King Burnaburiash I	1521–1503
King Assur-dan II	933–912	King Kashtiliash II	1502–1484
King Adadnirari II	911–891	King Agum III	1483–1465
King Tukulti-Ninurta II	890–885	King Karaindash	1445–1427
King Ashurnasirpal II	884–860	King Kurigalza III	1344–1320
King Shalmaneser III	859–825	King Nazimaruttash II	1319–1294

King Kadashman-Turgu	1293–1277	King Shalmaneser V	727–723
King Kadashman-Enlil II	1276–1271	King Merodach (Marduk-baladan III	722–710
King Kudur-Enlil	1270–1263	King Sargon II	710–705
King Sagarakti-Suriash	1262–1250	King Sennacherib	705–682
King Kastiash III	1249–1242	King Esarhaddon	681–669
King Adad-shum-nasir	1232–1203	King Shamash-shuma-ukin	668–648
King Melishipah II	1202–1188	King Kandalanu	648–627
King Merodach (Marduk)-baladan I	1187–1175	King Nabopolassar	626–605
King Zabada-sum-iddin	1174	King Nebuchadnezzer II	605–562
King Enlil-nadin-ahe	1173–1171	King Evil-Merodach (Amel-Marduk)	562–560
King Merodash (Marduk)-shapik-zer	1170–1153	King Nergal-shar-usur	559–556
King Ninurta-nadin-shumi	1152–1147	King Nabonidus	556–539
King Nebuchadnezzar	1146–1123	King Belshazzar	539–538
King Enlil-nadin-apli	1122–1117		
King Merocach (Marcuk)-nadin-ahe	1116–1101		
King Itti-Marduk-batatu	1100–1092	**Modern Iraq**	**A.D.**
King Merocach (Marduk)-shapik-zer-mati	1091–1084	King Faisal I	1921–1933
King Adad-apal-iddin	1083–1062	King Ghazi	1933–1939
King Nabo-Mukin-apli	990–955	King Faisal II	1939–1958
King Ninurta-kadur-usur	954	Regent Abdullah	1939–1953
King Marbiti-ahe-iddin	953–942	**(A Military republic was declared in 1958)**	
King Samas-mudaminiq	941–901	President Salam Muhammad Arif	1963–1966
King Nabo-shum-ukin	900–886	President Abdul Rahman Arif	1966–1968
King Nabo-apal-iddin	885–852	President Ahmad Hasan al-Bakr	1968–1979
King Merodach (Marduk)-zakir-shum	851–828	President Saddam Hussein	1979–
King Merodach (Marduk)-balatsuiqbi	827–815		
King Bau-ahe-iddin	814–811		
King Eriba-Marduk	802–763		
King Nabonassar	747–734		
King Nadinu	734–733		
King Ukin-zer	732–730		
King Tiglathpilser III	729–728		

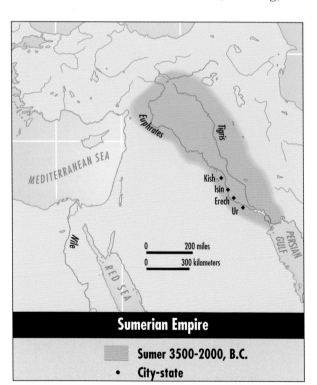

A stone carving that illustrates Sumerian tools

Sumerian Empire

Sumer 3500-2000, B.C.

• **City-state**

Sumerian Civilization

Sometime between 3500 and 3000 B.C., a group of people called Sumerians gathered along the rivers of southern Iraq and formed city-states. The Sumerian civilization developed many inventions that we now take for granted—such as the wheel, writing, counting, and calendars.

Perhaps the climate became drier than it had been, making the river waters even more valuable. Their spring floods enriched the soil each year. Sumerians dug canals that carried water to fields several miles from the rivers.

The Sumerians also developed plows. Perhaps the first plow was a crooked tree branch, but later plows were made of bronze. They used oxen to pull the plows and even made a planter by attaching a funnel for seeds. These improvements in farming were important to the development of civilization because they freed some people for other kinds of work.

The first wheel was solid, without any spokes. The wheel was also used as a disk by potters. The potter rotated the disk to shape a round pot. Wheels on carts and sails on boats meant that goods and supplies could be moved farther and faster. Metals were not found in the south, so farmers began trading with the mountain people for tin and copper to make bronze.

The Sumerians wondered why they had good crops in some years but were washed out or lacked enough water at other times. They came to believe that thousands of gods and goddesses controlled all of life and nature. They thought the gods made humans out of clay to serve as their slaves.

The Sumerians used plows and other "modern" inventions.

Your Mark—Cylinder Seals

Because most people could not read or write, they used seals to identify what they owned. People made their mark by rolling these cylinder seals with carved designs on wet clay. They also signed contracts with their seals. The seals varied in size from 1 to 3 inches (2.5 to 8 cm) in length. Their thickness ranged from the width of a pencil to that of a thumb. The cylinder was pierced lengthwise so that it could be worn on a string around the neck. Today, scholars study the designs on these seals to learn more about the lives of the people.

The temples to the gods became the most important buildings in the cities. Like Sumerian houses, temples were built of mud bricks on platforms. The mud frequently required rebuilding after rains, so the temples began to tower over the other buildings. Eventually, as the city-states grew, the temples were built very tall with steps leading up to a sanctuary on top. These temples are called ziggurats. At important feasts like New Year, the king climbed the steps to ask the goddess to grant a good harvest.

As the temples grew in size and influence, they created the need for specialized jobs—priests and priestesses, administrators, worship leaders, artists, musicians, cooks, weavers, and field-workers. Around 3000 B.C., one of the temples was said to be giving bread and beer to 1,200 people a day.

Perhaps the most remarkable inventions of the Sumerians were writing and counting. Writing on small clay tablets with a reed, they found it hard to make curved lines. They solved the problems by using a system of straight lines called cuneiform writing, a Latin word meaning "wedge-shaped." Versions of cuneiform writing were later used by other nations and existed as late as the first century A.D.

The Sumerians were also the first people to realize that the word two can apply to two of anything—apples and oranges, cows and buildings. The mathematical system they developed was based on the numeral 60. Sixty could be divided by twelve other numbers. The sixty-minute hour and the 360° circle are traced to the Sumerians.

To produce scribes who could handle words and figures, schools were established. Probably only the sons of wealthy families had the chance to go to school. Memorizing and

Some examples of cuneiform writing

Today children can go to school for free; for Sumerians, only the wealthy sons could attend.

copying lists seems to have accounted for much of the school day, which lasted from sunrise to sunset. Students who misbehaved were beaten with a stick. We have records of students playing hooky and of a father seeking a teacher's favor for his son by providing gifts.

This stone carving is actually a list of fields and estates, noting measurements and statistics.

Kings governed the city-states, which consisted of the city itself, plus the suburbs, nearby towns, gardens, palm groves, and grain fields around them. Lagash, one of the largest, covered 1,800 square miles (4,662 sq km) and had a population of 30,000 to 35,000.

The bottom rung of society consisted of slaves. Some slaves were prisoners of war and some were Sumerians who sold themselves or their children because of poverty. This group was never very large. Then there were landless workers employed by the temple or palace. On top was a large group of landowners, ranging from clothing merchants to the royal family. At first, the ruler did not hold that job for life, so councils of elders had an important role in government. Indeed, the idea of freedom was first expressed by the Sumerians.

As the kings gained greater power, however, they held their position for life, chose their own successor, and had many peo-

ple working for them. They had to collect taxes, make laws, and attend to canals and roads. Some cities even had a type of postal service. The gold and silver objects found in the Royal Tombs of Ur tell us that the kings lived in great luxury.

A Sumerian king on his throne

The Girl Who Was Late for Her Funeral

The Royal Tombs of Ur is one of the great archaeological finds. Helmets, crowns, statues, and harps (right) give a clue to the splendor in which the rulers lived. These tombs also contain the remains of some seventy-four soldiers and court ladies who accompanied the king. These people were beautifully dressed and apparently were drugged or poisoned from cups found near their skeletons. One of the court ladies was not wearing a headband like all the others, but a silver band was discovered nearby. The archaeologists wondered if she had been late for her own funeral and did not have time to take the headband out of her pocket. Nowhere else, with one possible exception, has a burial quite like this been found. Perhaps killing the attendants was not customary among the Sumerians.

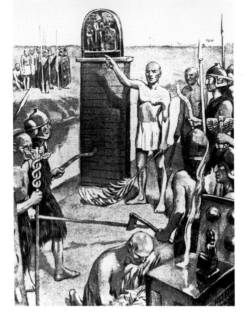

A battle over boundaries

The constant and ruthless warfare of the city-states eventually led to the downfall of the Sumerian civilization. Soon a group of people called the Akkadians took over the territory of Sumer and extended its boundaries.

Akkadian Civilization

The Akkadian language was completely different from the Sumerian—as different as Latin is from Chinese—but the Akkadians adapted the cuneiform system of writing to their language. Had the Akkadians always lived with the Sumerians? Or were they enemies, invaders, or nomads? Nobody knows.

Sargon the Great (about 2334–2279 B.C.)

Sargon rose from humble origins to become cupbearer to the Sumerian king of Kish, a city-state. According to legend, Sargon was born in secret. He was then placed in a reed basket sealed with bitumen (a tarlike substance), and floated down a river, where he was discovered by a man who raised him as his son.

After his first victory, the conquest of the Sumerian king of Umma, Sargon went on to carve out an empire. He washed his weapons symbolically in the Persian Gulf, indicating that he had conquered the south. Then he headed north to the Mediterranean. Next he fought to the east of Sumer. The statues and pillars inscribed with these conquests stop before the end of his reign.

He kept a large court at which he claimed 5,400 persons ate daily. Not far from Kish where he began his career, he built his capital called Agade.

The Akkadian rule lasted only about two hundred years, but it unified the country and pushed its boundaries out to the Mediterranean Sea and down to the Persian Gulf. The city-states were no longer the major political unit. Sargon the Great, king of the Akkadians, gave the Mesopotamians a taste for empire.

The Akkadian Empire changed the history of the area. The city-states lost their importance. The Akkadian language, art, and legends spread throughout the empire.

Neo-Sumerian Period

King Ur-Nammu sacrificing before a god

The Akkadians were overcome by the Guti, a people who ruled for about one hundred years. Not much is known about this period. After the Akkadians, however, the Sumerian city of Ur flourished again under the leadership of Ur-Nammu, who restored law and order. His reign gave us what is considered the earliest collection of laws. He built many structures in the city including a great ziggurat. Another builder of this era was Gudea, who erected temples and left behind many statues of himself.

The son and grandson of Ur-Nammu ruled over an empire at least as large as the Akkadian Empire had been, but better controlled. The kings formed administrative units, sent out royal inspectors, and separated military power from political power. Royal messengers and traders traveled on roads guarded by fortresses.

Gudea

However, the Amorites, who were considered barbarians by the Sumerians, began to attack the frontier. Suddenly, the empire began to break apart. Nomads continued to pour into the land and establish power bases. The old order collapsed along with Sumer, its city-states, and its powerful gods. Sumerian culture lived on in the language and literature.

For about two centuries around 2000–1800 B.C., the land was split into four factions. In the south, the kingdoms of Isin and Larsa challenged Ur for control over Sumer and Akkad. In the north, two other factions fought for control of the profitable trade routes. At last, Hammurabi, king of Babylon, conquered the four kingdoms, unified Mesopotamia, and founded the next great empire.

Hammurabi receiving law from the hand of the sun god

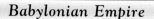

Babylonian Empire

Hammurabi inherited a small kingdom surrounded by more powerful states. During his reign from 1792 to 1750 B.C., however, he conquered the other Mesopotamian kingdoms, established Babylon as his capital, and took the title, King of the Four Quarters of the World.

Although we do not know the extent of his empire, we have a better idea of life in Babylon under Hammurabi than we have of life in some European countries only a thousand years ago. Libraries of clay tablets as well as monuments tell us that Hammurabi was a skilled diplomat, concerned for justice and the welfare of his people.

Code of Hammurabi

Although this code is no longer considered the oldest collection of laws in existence, it is the most complete of its time. It is not a group of statutes adopted by some legislature; it is a collection of the king's decisions. Toward the end of his reign, Hammurabi ordered these laws carved on stone and placed in temples to show that he had administered justice. The code dealt with at least 282 decisions and called for harsher punishment than was customary with the Sumerians. Now death, mutilation (such as putting out an eye), and corporal punishment (such as beatings) replaced the previous law that ordered compensation in terms of goods. Also, the punishments differed depending whether the victim was a free person, a state worker, or a slave. However, the main purpose of the code was to promote justice and prevent the strong from harming the weak.

The government established by Hammurabi exerted tight control over provincial governors, but each city had an assembly of elders who dealt with local matters and the collection of taxes. The Babylonian god Marduk, previously a minor deity, was promoted to chief god. In return, Hammurabi repaired the temples and treated the old traditions and myths with respect, adapting them to build his royal power.

Marduk

The reconstructed remains of a temple in Babylon

Ancient Babylonian ruins

The king was now the center of power. The palace, which had been fairly modest, became a huge complex of living quarters, office space, state reception rooms, and storage areas surrounded by walls for defense.

The towns and lifestyle of ordinary citizens then were not too different from those in older sections of Iraq today. Shops were clustered together as they are now in a modern souk, or shopping center. The mud-and-brick houses were plastered and whitewashed and had an inside courtyard. The family lived in the upper story, while visitors and servants used the ground floor. It is a design well suited to the climate.

Toward the end of his reign, Hammurabi boasted that he had made an end of war, promoted the welfare of his people, and allowed no one to terrorize them. However, the country's peace and prosperity may have depended too much on the personality of one man. The centralization of power may have come too fast.

When Hammurabi died in 1750 B.C., the empire began to disintegrate. Eventually, the kingdom fell to a new group of people—the Hittites. The Hittite conqueror did not establish a permanent settlement at Babylon. Instead another group of people, the Kassites, took control.

We know little about the Kassite era, which lasted some four hundred years. The Kassite rulers signed treaties dividing the country into two parts—Assyria in the north and Babylonia in the south. While Babylon lost political importance, it gained cultural status. Its literature was translated into the languages of countries throughout the Near East. From what is now Turkey to Egypt, the Babylonian language was used by diplomats.

Nebuchadrezzar I

In the north, the Assyrians managed to shake free from foreign domination. They controlled the plains and the trade routes to the Mediterranean countries, and planned to take over Babylonia to the south. Nebuchadrezzar I (sometimes referred to as Nebuchadnezzar) attacked and conquered Elam. He brought back to Babylon the

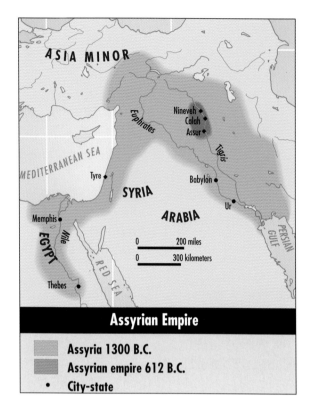

Assyrian Empire

▨ Assyria 1300 B.C.
▨ Assyrian empire 612 B.C.
• City-state

statue of the god Marduk that the Elamites had taken. However, Elam was not really conquered, and Nebuchadrezzar's successors had to worry about defense against their northern neighbor, Assyria.

Assyria was surrounded by enemies, but one of the great kings—Tiglathpileser I—managed to push them back, conquer Syria, and reach the Mediterranean Sea. However, the murder of this king was followed by several centuries of troubles and increasing occupation by the Aramaeans.

Assyrian Empire

At the end of the 1000s B.C., Assyria did not look like the great empire it was to become. Only the chaos among its enemies had preserved the country. The nation had lost a great deal of its territory, including the income-producing trade routes. And the tents of the Aramaeans almost reached the gates of Assur, the capital.

How did Assyria grow to become a great empire? First, it controlled its main cities. Its fighting forces were the best in the world—after all, they had been fighting almost as long as Assyria existed. They had chariots, horses, and weapons. Unlike their neighbors, they had a ruling dynasty that had been in power for some two centuries.

The Assyrians had several motives for waging war. They wanted to defend themselves. They wanted the loot and tribute they gained from the countries they conquered. They wanted their god, Assur, to be recognized as the most powerful. While a policy of terror was common among ancient conquerors, the Assyrians' boasts of torture put them in a class by themselves.

The king, Ashurnasirpal II, began a great building effort, not only in Assur and Nineveh but also with a strategically placed palace at what is now Nimrud. He brought back plants and animals from his expeditions. The huge palace at Nimrud, excavated by archaeologists, covered more than 6 acres (2.4 ha) and provided rooms for ceremonial, administrative, and living quarters. There was even a kind of air-conditioning system in the living quarters—vents were cut into walls to permit air circulation. A great banquet was held when the palace was opened in 879 B.C., with 69,574 guests being fed for ten days.

Sir Austen Henry Layard, an English archaeologist, led excavations of Nimrud.

Stone carvings found at Nimrud

King Sargon II

The palace at Nineveh

The son of Ashurnasirpal II, Shalmaneser III, carried on the family tradition of war by fighting for thirty-one of his thirty-five years on the throne. A 6-foot (2-m) obelisk of black alabaster, topped by a miniature ziggurat, depicts some of the king's victories. It shows the tribute paid by other monarchies, such as King Jehu of Israel. Jehu is the first Biblical person listed by name in the cuneiform inscriptions.

Tiglathpileser III was another powerful Assyrian ruler. He strengthened the royal power by reducing the authority of his lords. Provinces were treated like Assyrian districts, or allowed to keep their own rulers under royal supervisor. A standing army and a good system of communication with the provinces were also established. Masses of people were exiled to prevent revolts.

Sargon II, another great Assyrian king, strengthened the empire. He built a huge palace-temple complex close to Nineveh, near what is now the village of Khorsabad. The ziggurat was seven stories high—each level painted a different

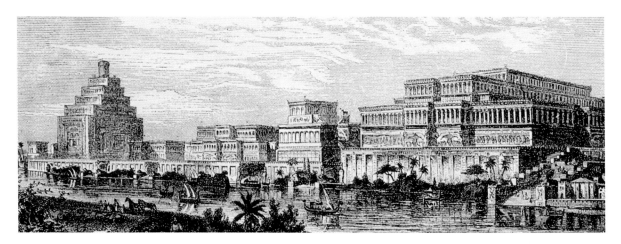

color and encircled with a spiral ramp. The complex was scarcely occupied, however before it was abandoned. Sargon II was killed in battle and his successor moved elsewhere.

Sargon's heir, Sennacherib, is known for his attack on Judah in Palestine. He captured Lachish and laid siege to Jerusalem. Hezekiah, strengthened by the prophet Isaiah, did not surrender, but the Assyrians withdrew with valuable tribute from Judah. On his way to attack Egypt, Sennacherib's army was hit by a plague that killed thousands of troops, according to Hebrew scripture. In 689 B.C., Sennacherib put down a revolt in Babylon and unlike previous rulers who had treated Babylon as the second city of the empire, he destroyed the town. In Assyria, he made Nineveh the capital city. Its water system of canals and aqueducts was an engineering marvel.

Esarhaddon, who took over after the death of Sennacherib, was known for rebuilding Babylon and for his attacks on Egypt. He captured the royal palace at Memphis. When he died on his way back from Egypt, his two sons took over. Ashurbanipal was to rule in the north, and his brother, Shamash-shuma-ukin, was to govern Babylon without dividing the empire. Twice Ashurbanipal conquered Egypt, but he was a long way from Assyria in a strange land with its own language, religion, and customs. Although he left local governors in charge, the Egyptians regained power. When Shamash-shuma-ukin, who had cooperated for seventeen years, decided to claim the territory around Babylon, Ashurbanipal returned home and conquered Babylon.

Inside an Assyrian palace

An Assyrian clay tablet

The Assyrian civilization had many achievements beyond perfecting the arts of war and administration. Their sculpture provided humans with a lesson in political propaganda, and their collections and translations of tablets are impressive. The Assyrians attempted to classify natural phenomena; their knowledge of mathematics, astronomy, and medicine is truly remarkable. Indeed, an Assyrian map has been found on which the country farthest to the north is called the "land where the sun is not seen," which leads one to wonder: how did the Assyrians know about Arctic winters?

In spite of their great achievements, the Assyrian Empire collapsed suddenly in 612 B.C.—only twenty-seven years after Ashurbanipal celebrated his triumph over the city of Susa as the most powerful leader. When he died, his two sons fought for the throne. The Medes and Chaldeans, who had taken over Babylon, attacked Assyria and destroyed its major cities. In three years, they managed to conquer an empire that had dominated this part of the world for three centuries.

Chaldean or Neo-Babylonian Civilization

The Medes took their loot from the fighting and left the Chaldeans in control of Assyria. However, the Chaldeans made no effort to rebuild the cities in the north. They put all their effort into a religious and cultural revival in the south. Babylon was now the capital of their empire. They were concerned about Egyptian influence in the area of Syria and Palestine, which blocked their trade opportunities with the West. Their king, Nebuchadrezzar II, defeated the Egyptians, and on March 16, 597 B.C., he captured Jerusalem. Some three thousand Jews were deported to Babylon.

Nebuchadrezzar II

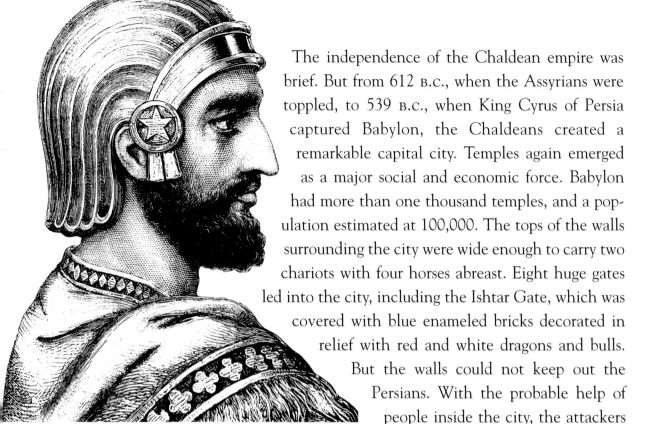

King Cyrus of Persia

The independence of the Chaldean empire was brief. But from 612 B.C., when the Assyrians were toppled, to 539 B.C., when King Cyrus of Persia captured Babylon, the Chaldeans created a remarkable capital city. Temples again emerged as a major social and economic force. Babylon had more than one thousand temples, and a population estimated at 100,000. The tops of the walls surrounding the city were wide enough to carry two chariots with four horses abreast. Eight huge gates led into the city, including the Ishtar Gate, which was covered with blue enameled bricks decorated in relief with red and white dragons and bulls. But the walls could not keep out the Persians. With the probable help of people inside the city, the attackers surprised the defenders.

The large throne room in the palace seems to have been decorated with animals and flowers to create beauty, rather than the massive bull-men of the Assyrians designed to inspire awe and fear. In one part of the palace area, three well shafts, probably used with a chain pump, have been discovered. Could these have watered the famous Hanging Gardens of Babylon, one of the Seven Wonders of the Ancient World? Records from that time tell us that these gardens were built by Nebuchadrezzar for his wife, the Median princess Amytis, who was homesick for the green plants of her homeland.

All this building put a heavy load of taxes on the people. A system of standardized money based on silver made it possible to borrow funds. Private business flourished, creating great power for some families. The temples became important economic units and were able to keep the civilization alive even after Babylon fell to the Persians. The Persians tried to return the city to normal functioning after the war. Cyrus proclaimed himself ruler and worshiped the Babylon god, Marduk. Babylon continued to be a great city, if not the capital of an empire. In A.D. 600s, it was abandoned and finally buried beneath the sands.

The wall and Hanging Gardens of Babylon

Decline and Death of the Ancient Mesopotamian Civilization

Opposite: **Alexander the Great conquering Babylon**

Throughout this long period of history—down to the 539 B.C. capture of Babylon by Cyrus of Persia—a flow of ideas and customs had developed in the Land between Two Rivers. Now under foreign control, Mesopotamia lost out to other countries and eventually became forgotten.

The Achaemenian, or Persian Period, began in 539 B.C., with the new kings still performing some royal duties. However, the successors to Cyrus were more concerned with fighting the Egyptians, and then the Greeks. The Persians made Aramaic the language of their empire. Soon, only scholars and scribes could read the Akkadian and Sumerian languages in the cuneiform script. Thus, the common people lost their native language—and the key to their history.

Alexander the Great brought the Greek Empire to the region, beginning the Hellenistic Period. The Persian armies surrendered Babylon without a fight. Alexander was greeted as a liberator and accepted as a king. He offered sacrifices to Marduk and ordered the rebuilding of the temples, although this task was not completed. He planned to make the city one of the capitals of his empire and a great port after he made the Euphrates River navigable to the Persian Gulf. But Alexander's death in Babylon at the age of thirty-two in 323 B.C., probably from malaria, cut short these dreams.

Alexander's successors were not able to hold his empire together. The Greeks founded their own cities in the area, and the center of culture and political importance shifted to

The ruins at Ctesiphon

the Mediterranean. However, the temples continued to preserve the ancient learning.

Then the territory was claimed by the Parthians with control established around 122 B.C. In A.D. 200s, the Sassanians of Persia took over. They developed a centralized control of the river systems for irrigation and travel, and built the city of Ctesiphon on the trade routes between East and West. The remains of its palace with the arch of the huge vaulted hall still impress travelers. The Romans captured the city twice, but were unable to hold it. The Sassanians attempted to force their own faith on the people in this area. They attacked the Jews and Christians who were living in this territory. However, it was the new religion of Islam that overwhelmed this empire and started a new era for this ancient country.

Arab Conquest

The Arabs, inspired by the teachings of Muhammad, the prophet of Islam, conquered the Persians in A.D. 637. When Muhammad, who lived in the territory that is now Saudi Arabia, died in 632, there was a crisis about who should be his successor. Several of the competing factions accepted sixty-year-old Abu Bakr, the prophet's earliest follower outside of his family. He was given the title of caliph, meaning successor. Others felt that the title should have gone to the nearest male relative, Muhammad's cousin and son-in-law, Ali, who had married Muhammad's daughter Fatimah and fathered the only grandsons of the prophet. This dispute has had a long-lasting effect to today, because it split Islam into the two largest branches: the Sunnis and the Shiites.

When Abu Bakr died, Umar ibn al-Khattab became caliph and declared the mission of Islam to be a holy war against people who practiced other religions. The tough Arab fighters were small in numbers, but they outmaneuvered the Byzantine and Persian empires, taking both Jerusalem and Ctesiphon in the year 637 and pressing on into India. Umar, stabbed to death by a Persian slave, was succeeded by Uthman, who founded the Umayyad dynasty.

The first revolt against Uthman came in what is now Iraqi territory at Kufa near Ctesiphon, where he was killed. The next caliph chosen was Ali, who had lost the first election. near Ctesiphon, where he was killed. The next caliph chosen was Ali, who had lost the first election.

Two important battles involving Ali were fought on what is now Iraqi soil. In the Battle of the Camel near Basra, he defeated his opponents who included Muhammad's widow, Alishah. It was the first major clash between Muslims. The second battle was fought on the plain of Siffin on the Euphrates against forces of a relative of Uthman, Muawiyah. Ali, beaten in the fight, was forced to submit the matter to arbitration, and had to retreat to Kufa. Ali lost prestige, and, in 661, a group of former supporters killed him.

Muawiyah put himself forward as a candidate to be the next caliph. When Ali's eldest son was persuaded to give up his claim, Muawiyah became the first caliph in the Umayyad line to rule from Damascus in what is now Syria. The boundaries of the Umayyads stretched from China across North Africa and up through Spain to within 100 miles (160 km) of Paris, France.

The Umayyads still faced controversy. Ali's second son, Hussein, the only living grandson of the prophet Muhammad, was trying to join some rebels in what is now Iraq. In 680, near the city of Karbala, they were wiped out by government forces. Hussein's head was cut off and sent to Damascus. This act led to the formation of a political party that opposed the Umayyads. The party, known as the Shiat Ali or Party of Ali, became the Shiites, one of the two largest divisions in Islam. The other group, the Sunnis, are the largest.

Another challenge of the caliphate came at a time of increasing unhappiness with the worldliness of the Umayyads. The family descended from Abbas claimed power and leadership of the Sunnis. Abbas was the uncle of Muhammad, and therefore a proper candidate from the Shiite view that the caliph should be from the prophet's family. In 750 the Abbasids, as the family was known, overthrew the Umayyads and transferred the capital of their empire from Damascus to Baghdad.

The Abbasids

Abu al-Abbas founded a line of rulers that lasted until 1258. His caliphate was a return to the religiously oriented state from the more secular one of his predecessors.

The successor to Abbas, Abu Ja'far, known as al-Mansur, established Baghdad as his capital. Within a century, that city was estimated to have a population of a million. The city was built on a circular plan with three walls and a double moat.

The Thousand and One Nights

For centuries, people have been fascinated by the stories of life at this time as recorded in *The Thousand and One Nights* (sometimes called the *Arabian Nights*). According to that classic, a beautiful girl, Scheherazade, was able to save her life by telling her husband such wonderful stories that he could not kill her until he heard the ending the following night, at which time she started a new story. From this book, we have the tales of "Aladdin and the Magic Lamp" (the film *Aladdin*, left), "Ali Baba and the Forty Thieves," "The Voyages of Sinbad the Sailor," and many others.

A view of the city and harbor of Baghdad

The caliph's palace had a golden dome and a golden gate. The palace boasted a solid silver tree with branches of silver and gold, on which mechanical birds sang. The branches moved as if a breeze were blowing.

Baghdad was also the intellectual capital of the world. It reached its height under the well-known Caliph Harun al-Rashid in the 700s at a time when Europe was still in the Dark Ages. Scholars could consult translations from Greek, Persian, and Indian sources. Theology and law were important studies. Medicine and pharmacology made significant gains. Hospitals were established at Baghdad and in the provinces. Scholars studied astronomy and mathematics as well as music, poetry, and art.

Baghdad became the center for Middle Eastern trade. Merchants placed their products on ships that sailed to India, Ceylon (now Sri Lanka), and China. Camel caravans took land routes to Baghdad from Persia, Arabia, Egypt, Syria, and beyond. However, the old pattern of inner divisions and rebellions in the provinces repeated itself. Religious persecutions began against Muslim groups considered unorthodox and against Jews and Christians.

The Buyids, a Shiite family of Persian origin, seized power while leaving the Sunni caliph in place. These rulers were unable to prevent outsiders from attacking Baghdad and terrorizing the residents. It was then that a Sunni family of Turkish origin, the Seljuqs, took over. Toghril Beg conquered Baghdad in 1055 and ousted the Buyids by 1059. In an effort to restore orthodoxy, the Sunni family founded colleges for the training of officials in religious and secular matters. Shiite families had strong local power in the south. Religious disputes and power plays further weakened central control. Although the Crusades from the nations of the West had been successfully repelled, a new threat came from another direction—the Mongols.

Conquerors from Outside

The grandson of Genghis Khan, Hulago, conquered Baghdad in 1258 after a siege of seven weeks. The city was sacked, and large numbers of people were put to death. Artistic and cultural treasures were destroyed or stolen. The country was devastated and unable to regain its strength until the twentieth century.

Another band of Mongols under Tamerlane (also called Timur) conquered Baghdad in 1393 and again in 1401. The city suffered another siege of destruc-

The siege of Baghdad in 1258

Suleyman captured Baghdad
for the Ottoman Empire.

tion and killing. Throughout this period of chaos, Bedouin people in the south and tribes of Turkomans and Kurds in the north revolted against outside power. Religious tensions among the groups continued with different factions attempting to seize control. Meanwhile, the strong Ottoman Turkish Empire building in the West extended its control over the area. The great Ottoman leader, Suleyman the Magnificent, captured Baghdad in the 1530s. Except for a brief period of Persian control, the Ottomans held the land that was to become Iraq until 1918.

Gaining control over the various tribal leaders was the work of one of the strongest governors, Midhat Pasha, who governed Iraq from 1869 to 1872. He brought in reforms providing a voice for local people in government, and establishing a system of education outside the mosques and the settlement of tribes on specific land. He started newspapers, hospitals, and banks. The Western powers of Europe had begun to take an interest in the area, particularly Germany and Great Britain. When the Ottoman Turks sided with Germany in World War I, the British took over Baghdad, and announced their intention to give Iraqis some control over their country. The territory had been under foreign control since the Mongol invasion in the 1200s.

At the peace conferences following World War I, however, the Allied powers decided to divide up the former Ottoman territories between them. All the modern countries of the Fertile Crescent were set up with new boundaries. Iraq and Palestine were placed under British control, while Syria and Lebanon were given to the French. For three months, a revolt against the British caused turmoil in Iraq. In October 1920, a temporary Arab government was set up, answerable to the British high commissioner for Iraq, Sir Percy Cox. In a referendum, the people voted Prince Faisal to be their king. As a descendant of the prophet Muhammad and as one who had fought for Arab nationalism, he had the right background. In 1930, the British agreed by treaty to terminate their rule.

Signing the peace treaty at Versailles, following World War I

Prince Faisal became king of Iraq in 1921.

The Monarchy

Iraq became an independent state in 1932. With the discovery of oil and the export of oil products by 1930, the government now had revenues to work with.

Many of the traditional tensions between groups continued—town against tribe, merchants against debtors, Sunnis against Shiites. The problem of the Kurds increased. At the end of World War I, there had been a conditional agreement between the Allies and Turkey to establish an independent Kurdish state—Kurdistan—with territory taken from Iraq, Turkey, and Iran. However, because of changed political conditions in Turkey, the plan was not put into effect. In 1926 when the League of Nations awarded the city of Mosul to Iraq rather than Turkey, the Kurdish areas were brought under Iraqi rule. Some Kurds have continued to demand the right to decide for themselves how they want to be governed.

King Faisal I ruled from 1921 to 1933. He was succeeded by his son, King Ghazi. As demands for government reforms and for improvement of conditions grew, the military began to take an active role in politics. In 1936, a military coup d'etat (overthrow of the government) forced out the elected officials but left the king in place. After several more such coups, the politicians and military split into two major groups. One was pro-British; the other pro-German.

In 1939, King Ghazi, who liked to drive fast cars, was killed in a car crash. He left the crown to his four-year-old son Faisal II, whose uncle, Abd al-Ilah, became the crown prince and regent to act for the boy.

King Ghazi standing before his airplane

During World War II (1939–45), the leader of the pro-German faction tried to seize the government and break a 1930 treaty with the British about wartime rights. The British landed military forces in Iraq, while the Iraqi army received some support from pro-German powers. The British put down the fighting. Afterwards, Iraq supported the Allies and declared war on Germany and its allies.

In 1945, Iraq was one of the founding members of the Arab League, which provided a loose framework for unity with other Arab nations. Also in 1945, Iraq joined the United Nations. When there was concern about the rising power of the Soviet Union, Iraq signed the Baghdad Pact, a mutual defense treaty with Turkey, and later with Iran and Pakistan. In 1958, Iraq joined with Jordan to form the Arab Federation, an organization designed to counter the anti-Western United Arab Republic formed earlier by Egypt and Syria.

Within Iraq, the two strong leaders were Nuri as-Said and Crown Prince Abd al-Ilah. King Faisal II came to power in 1953. Many of the leaders of reform movements felt that the

King Faisal II shaking hands with his uncle, Crown Prince Abd al-Ilah

Young King Faisal shortly before his monarchy was overthrown

Troops in the palace courtyard

Prime Minister Qasim
reviewing the troops

Abdul Rahman Arif (left)
with Ahmad Hasan al-Bakr

government was opposed to reform. Nuri as-Said banned all political parties in 1954. Opposition grew, especially after the French, British, and Israelis attacked Egypt in 1956. Many people resented the government's ties to the West because of Western support for Israel.

In the revolution of 1958, the monarchy was overthrown; Nuri as-Said, Crown Prince Abd al-Ilah, and King Faisal II, along with other members of the royal family, were killed. Two army officers, Brigadier General Abd al-Karim Qasim and Colonel Abdul Salam Arif, led the coup. Baghdad was captured on July 14, 1958.

The Revolutionaries

Qasim, as head of the Revolutionary Forces, formed a cabinet over which he presided. Iraq was declared a republic—no longer a monarchy headed by a king. Islam was the state religion. A constitution announced that Iraq was part of the Arab nation, with Arabs and Kurds as partners in the homeland. Arif, with whom Qasim had plotted to overthrow the old government, was soon out of favor. He was associated with the powerful Baath political party and was accused of plotting against the best interests of Iraq.

During the following years, Iraq came under pressure from various Iraqi groups and had a succession of leaders: Qasim (executed, 1963); Arif (killed in a helicopter crash, 1966); Abdul Rahman Arif (exiled, 1968); and General Ahmad Hasan al-Bakr (resigned, 1979). The West was hated for its support of Israel in the Arab–Israeli War of 1967.

Saddam Hussein

Saddam Hussein was born in 1937 to a poor family in Tikrit, Iraq. A Sunni Muslim, he claims descent from the prophet Muhammad. In 1959, he went into exile in Egypt after taking part in an unsuccessful attempt to assassinate President Qasim. He has tortured and killed political opponents—even members of his own family. He has used poison gas against the Kurds and Iranians. His eight-year war with Iran and his attempt to take over Kuwait have damaged his country. Yet he likes to think he is as great as Nebuchadrezzar II.

Saddam Hussein

On July 16, 1979, Saddam Hussein replaced Bakr as president and chairman of the Revolutionary Command Council. Hussein pleaded for Arab solidarity and saw himself as the leader of all Arabs.

Iraqi troops at war with Iran

Ayatollah Khomeini

In 1979, Iran had an Islamic revolution in which the Ayatollah Khomeini became the leader of the country. Khomeini, a Shiite, urged Iraqi Shiites and others to overthrow the Iraqi government. War with Iran began on September 16, 1980, with Iraq's forces entering Iran. Success in battle shifted back and forth until an inconclusive end was negotiated on August 20, 1988. It has been estimated that 150,000 Iraqis died during the eight-year war and many more were injured. The Shiite Iraqis remained loyal to their nation and suspicious of Khomeini.

When the war with Iran ended, Saddam Hussein turned his attention to the Kurds who had sided with Iran. Some 60,000 Kurds fled to Turkey for refuge and even more escaped to Iran. The Iraqi use of chemical warfare in the last days of the fighting against Iran, and then later against the Kurds, brought a strong international protest.

Then on August 2, 1990, Saddam Hussein invaded neighboring Kuwait. He claimed that Kuwait belonged to Iraq and was an Iraqi province. Other Arab nations did not support his invasion.

Hussein then moved his troops toward Saudi Arabia. By August 6, the U.N. Security Council had voted a trade embargo against goods entering Iraq and also placed an embargo on Iraq's oil exports, thus depriving Iraq of most of its

income. Saudi Arabia invited the United States and other nations to send troops to help defend Saudi territory. The troops arrived, calling their operation Desert Shield.

Saddam Hussein threatened to destroy Arab oil fields and attack Israel. On September 25, the U.N. Security Council

These Kurds had to flee to Turkey after they sided with Iran.

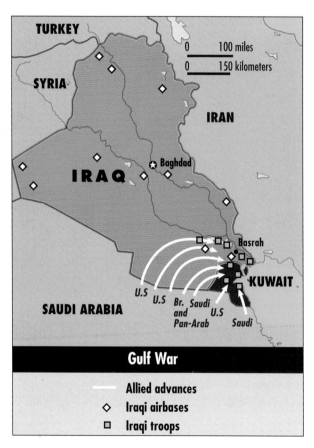

Gulf War

— Allied advances
◇ Iraqi airbases
□ Iraqi troops

voted to extend its land and sea embargo to include air traffic. The council also adopted resolutions condemning Iraq's takeover of Kuwait and ordered Iraq to withdraw its troops by January 15, 1991.

But Saddam Hussein did not withdraw his troops. On January 16, a multinational Allied force began missile attacks against Iraq. Operation Desert Shield became Desert Storm. Iraq responded by firing Scud missiles at Saudi Arabia and Israel.

On February 24, the Allies began a ground attack designed to retake Kuwait. The Iraqis gave little resistance. After one hundred hours, the Allies had pushed Iraqi forces out of Kuwait and secured a surrender. The Gulf War was over, but Saddam Hussein was still in power. Many hoped that the Iraqi people would oust their leader, but after many unsuccessful assassination attempts and two revolts, he remains their president.

Both Kuwait and Iraq suffered severe destruction. Power, water, highway, and bridge facilities had been knocked out by air strikes on Iraq. Kuwait and other countries had to deal with the environmental disasters caused when Hussein released oil into the Persian Gulf and torched the oil fields.

Saddam Hussein then turned his attention to groups that might want to unseat him—the Kurds in the north and the Shiites in the south. Iraqi rebels clashed with the Iraqi army in a number of cities.

Because Saddam tried to attack these people by air, a no-fly zone was imposed by the U.N. on Iraqi forces, whereby Iraqi planes could not fly above the 36th parallel and below the 32nd parallel.

In 1994, Iraqi troops approached the Kuwait border again. The troops were withdrawn when the United States put armed forces in position. In 1995, Saddam held a vote on a seven-year term as president. He won 99.96 percent of the vote—with ballots that had to be

Opposite: **A young boy viewing the damage from a missile attack**

A row of stores destroyed by bombing

signed with the voter's name. Opposition groups claimed that the election had no meaning under such conditions. In 1996, the United States named Iraq as a sponsor of international terrorism.

Then, in the fall of 1996, one of two main Kurdish groups invited Saddam Hussein to help them defeat the other Kurdish group, which it claimed was getting help from Iran. Saddam responded and regained some control of the north through his Kurdish allies. He also threatened United States and Allied planes patrolling the no-fly zone by firing anti-aircraft guns against them. The United States responded with missiles that destroyed Iraqi military positions in the south. However, because Saddam acted within his own territory, other countries in the multinational force of the Gulf War refused to take action. The no-fly zone was increased to the 33rd parallel.

In 1997, the U.N. allowed Iraq to sell some oil for food, medicine, and other necessities to alleviate the suffering of the people. This lifting was initially rejected by Saddam Hussein as violating state

Saddam seems to be everywhere, even on the face of this watch.

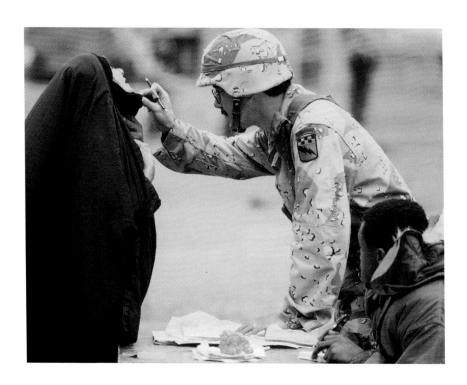

A U.S. doctor trying to help
an Iraqi civilian in 1991

sovereignty. He finally accepted it, and Iraq began exporting a
limited amount of oil under U.N. supervision. Iraq's leaders
have plenty of food and luxuries. It is the Iraqi people who
have gone hungry and have had to sell whatever they can to
get the necessities of life.

Iraq has not complied with the peace treaty requirement to
reveal information about Iraq's biological and chemical
weapons. When some of Saddam's relatives sought refuge in
Jordan and threatened to reveal the information, Saddam
became more cooperative. However, the relatives were killed
when they returned to Iraq.

In 1997, Saddam Hussein interfered with efforts by the
U.N. to check compliance with the destruction of chemical

and biological weapons by limiting access to locations, by thwarting U.N. surveillance equipment, and by trying to specify the nationality of U.N. personnel. Also, Saddam may have been trying to prevent the discovery of mass graves. Some 608 Kuwaitis taken by the Iraqis in the Gulf War had not been returned. More than 700 Iranian soldiers held as prisoners of war from the Iran–Iraq War had not been returned.

It was not the goal of the Persian Gulf War to remove Saddam Hussein. It was hoped that the Iraqis would kick him out and be able to set up a stable government. A strong Iraq provides some protection against Iran taking over the oil fields. Too strong an Iraq poses a threat to the oil fields in Kuwait and Saudi Arabia.

Getting basic items at the market has proven difficult during Saddam's reign.

A Dictator's Power

How do you describe a government that has—on paper—a constitution and democratic institutions, while in reality, one man's word controls the nation? John Deutch, director of the U.S. Central Intelligence Agency (CIA), in his report to Congress said: "There is no press freedom, and brutal suppression continues. Saddam Hussein's security apparatus has systematically destroyed all groups that have formed inside the country. People are arrested and killed."

76

T
HE COUNTRY THAT WAS THE FIRST TO develop the idea of freedom is now a country where freedom does not exist. It will help us understand the situation if we look first at the government as it appears on paper to see what might be available to the Iraqis if Saddam Hussein is ever overthrown. A second look will tell us what is really going on in Iraq under the control of a dictator.

Government on Paper

Iraq has had a constitution since 1968 that declares the country a republic, a democratic nation with Islam as the state religion. The economy is to be based on socialism (government ownership) rather than capitalism (private ownership). The government is to protect liberty of religion and freedom of speech and of opinion. Public meetings are allowed. Discrimination is not legal. Freedom of the press and the right to form societies and unions are guaranteed. The right to autonomy for the Kurdish people is recognized. A new

The Flag

The Iraqi flag's horizontal stripes are red for courage, white for generosity, and black for the conquests of Islam. On the white stripe are three stars and the words "God is Great" in Arabic script. These are written in green, the traditional color of Islam. The three stars represented Iraq, Syria, and Egypt when there was a plan for the three countries to unite. The plan failed. The flag was adopted in 1963, but the words were added during the Persian Gulf War in 1991.

Saddam Hussein won the 1995 election by a 99.96% vote.

permanent constitution was announced in 1989, adopted by the legislature in 1990, to be submitted to popular vote for approval.

The center of power is the president and the Revolutionary Command Council (RCC), which in 1997 had eight members. At present, the president and vice-president are elected by a two-thirds majority of the RCC. They are responsible to the RCC. The vice-president and a council of ministers (appointed by the president) are answerable to the president. Under the new, permanent constitution (not yet in force), the RCC is to be abolished following a presidential election and the creation of a 50-member Consultative Assembly together with the existing 250-member National Assembly.

Saddam Hussein is the president, chief of state, and head of government, the official supreme commander of the armed forces, the president of the RCC, secretary general of the Baath Party (the only political party in Iraq), and the prime minister. He has appointed three deputy prime ministers. In 1995, a popular vote was taken in which Saddam Hussein was approved by a 99.96 percent vote for a seven-year term.

Iraqi opposition groups outside the country claim that this vote had no meaning. Foreign observers noted that voters had to sign their names to the ballots.

The judicial system is supervised by a council headed by the minister of justice. There are three separate types of courts: civil, religious, and special. The civil courts hear both civil and criminal cases. Decisions can be appealed to higher courts. The highest civil court is the Court of Cassation, which also hears cases involving crimes committed by public officials. Each of the religious communities has its own court, which considers questions of personal status, marriage, and inheritance. Special courts have jurisdiction over cases involving state security.

Iraqis voting in 1995

After the Persian Gulf War, crime increased. Hussein ordered a return to the Islamic law of cutting off a hand at the wrist for stealing. This practice was later stopped because of protests.

The country has eighteen provinces. Each is headed by a governor who has broad powers. Three are designated as autonomous regions. In a 1974 attempt to end Kurdish fight-

ing, a constitutional amendment was introduced, providing that the area whose population is mainly Kurdish will enjoy autonomy as defined by law. A fifty-member Kurdish Legislative Council was established.

Kurds in northern Iraq

Government in Reality

How much freedom does an Iraqi really have to speak out in opposition to the government? One U.S. reporter visiting the country in 1988 told of the difficulty of finding anyone who would speak openly against Saddam Hussein. One person waited until everyone in his office left, then turned up the radio and whispered that his phone was tapped and the office was bugged. He said Saddam was the worst dictator in history and added that he could be shot for saying so. This man refused to put up all the usual pictures of Saddam, but he admitted that he kept a carpet in his closet that was decorated with the president's face. If the security police came to his door, he could quickly unroll the carpet so that he would appear to support Saddam.

While criticism of Saddam Hussein is not permitted, praise of him is encountered everywhere. Pictures of Saddam Hussein are seen everywhere throughout the country. More than two hundred songs have been written about him.

Nightly Praise of Saddam

The evening television news is said to begin with this chant:

"Oh Saddam, our victorious; Oh Saddam, our beloved;
You carry the nation's dawn between your eyes....
Oh Saddam, everything is good with you....
Allah, Allah, we are happy; Saddam lights our days."

Structure of national government

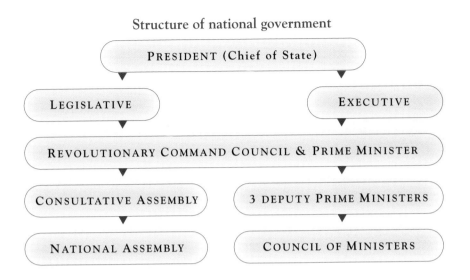

PRESIDENT (Chief of State)

LEGISLATIVE   EXECUTIVE

REVOLUTIONARY COMMAND COUNCIL & PRIME MINISTER

CONSULTATIVE ASSEMBLY   3 DEPUTY PRIME MINISTERS

NATIONAL ASSEMBLY   COUNCIL OF MINISTERS

The security or secret police are given a free hand in Iraq. The worst kind of torture has been reported over and over by Iraqis who have fled to a country where they can speak freely. The judges and courts are no protection. An Iraqi reported that a friend of his—a judge—was ordered to come to the security department in the middle of the night. He was told to issue some arrest warrants. When the judge asked what offense he should charge the people with, he was told to make up a charge. Then he asked to see the people who were to be arrested. The security police told him to hurry up and make out the warrants because the people had already been killed. The judge issued the warrants.

Can anything be done to help the Iraqis without interfering in their country? At least those who have escaped from Iraq can tell their stories. The more that is known of the situation, the better the chances for change. Apparently, the most

Uday Hussein (above right) and his younger brother have been involved in the Iraqi government. Uday was in charge of information, culture, and youth. Uday has three sisters, and some of their husbands also had government positions before they were executed.

Uday was born in 1964. Unlike most Iraqis who name their children after Islamic heroes, Saddam (above left) gave his sons names from the pre-Islamic period. Sons are supposed to carry on the family traditions.

A number of scandals have become associated with Uday. There are two versions of the killing of one of Saddam's most valuable bodyguards, Kamel Hanna Jejjo, in 1988. According to one account Jejjo was intoxicated and started firing randomly in the air with his submachine gun. This common way of celebrating was banned recently when several people were hit during the celebration of the cease-fire in the war with Iran as the rounds fell

back to earth. Uday ordered Jejjo to stop firing. When Jejjo did not, Uday raised a stick to hit him across the shoulders. Unfortunately, Jejjo stepped back. The blow landed on his head, and he died the next morning.

The other version of the story is that Uday was intoxicated and shooting off his gun, and that Uday hit Jejjo with a tire iron when Jejjo had tried to make him stop. Saddam was furious with his son. He was concerned about the attitude of the other bodyguards. Moreover, Jejjo was the son of Saddam's personal cook and had been Saddam's food taster. Obviously, Uday would have to be punished. The son was at first put in prison—and later released. Many of his official positions were taken away. The matter was investigated by the justice minister. Finally, Jejjo's father asked that the charges be dropped.

Previously that year, Uday had wanted to buy some $40,000 worth of handguns from the United States. The export license was refused because Iraq and Iran were at war.

Then in January 1989, Uday was sent to Geneva, Switzerland, with a relative. Within a short time, Uday pulled a knife on a Swiss policeman in an argument in a restaurant. He was promptly asked to leave the country.

In 1995, Saddam Hussein ordered his son never to appear in his presence with a gun. The father ordered the destruction of several dozen of his son's sports cars. It has been said that it was Uday's violent behavior that prompted Saddam's daughters and sons-in-law to flee to Jordan.

Uday, himself, was the victim of an attack in December 1996, in which he was seriously wounded.

A Look at Baghdad, Iraq's Capital

Baghdad, the capital city of Iraq, was founded in A.D. 762 on the west bank of the Tigris River by al-Mansur, the second Caliph of the Abbasid dynasty. The part of the city that soon sprang up on the east bank of the Tigris became Baghdad's major district. Baghdad was known as the City of Peace or the Round City for the fortification that encircled the ancient city-center. Baghdad reached its intellectual and commercial height in the 700s and 800s under Caliphs Mahdi and Harun al-Rashid, and became the center of Islam when Islamic civilization was at its peak. The average temperature in Baghdad is 93°F (34°C) in the summer and 52°F (11°C) in the winter. Its population is estimated at approximately 4 million.

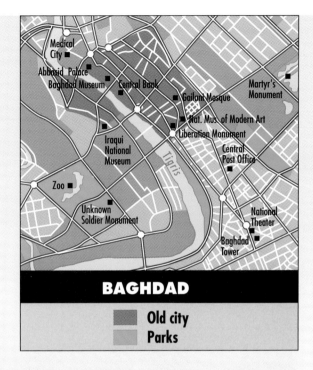

BAGHDAD

Old city
Parks

likely way to overthrow Saddam Hussein is a coup by the army officers around him. Past attempts have failed, however, and even the suspicion of a threat to Saddam Hussein has caused the person to be killed.

It would seem that Saddam Hussein is fearful even of his favorite son, Uday Hussein—perhaps with good reason.

Before the long war with Iran and the air strikes of Desert Storm, Baghdad was described by some as the most exciting city of the Near East—better than Damascus in Syria or Cairo in Egypt. Now, sanctions and government repression have made life difficult there.

Baghdad is a modern city with many neighborhoods or districts. It has a diverse population of ethnic groups. It is a center for culture, trade, and transportation. The city's, shrines, mosques (Islamic places of worship), schools, palaces, and eight museums display beautiful architecture.

C H A P T E R

S I X

Oil and Food

Iraq is an oil-rich country with a sizable educated population. It has all the resources needed for developing a strong economy. Instead, Saddam Hussein's wars have not given the Iraqis the chance to enjoy the full benefits of their land. In addition, an estimated $2.7 billion was spent in 1994 on the armed forces.

THE NATION'S INFRASTRUCTURE—the power, water, highways, bridges, and communications systems on which industry relies—was severely damaged by bombs. Much of this infrastructure has since been rebuilt.

Roads, bridges, and buildings were damaged during the Persian Gulf War.

But the debt that Iraq must now pay to others is immense. The country owes huge sums for damage to Kuwaiti citizens, for wrecking Kuwaiti petroleum facilities, and for paying what is

Iraqi troops proved expensive and increased the country's debt.

owed to foreign workers who had to leave Kuwait. Before the Persian Gulf War, Iraq's foreign debt of $75 billion was considered a serious problem. Now its debt is estimated at $200 billion.

Iraq's people have not been able to get the food to which they were accustomed, but they are being fed. Saddam Hussein and his ruling class, however, have not had to face shortages.

The U.N. applied sanctions so others would not trade with Iraq, hoping to force Saddam to withdraw from Kuwait and later to comply with the terms of surrender. These sanctions have remained in force because he has not turned over required information about armaments or met the other terms. At the end of 1996, Iraq began exporting a limited amount of oil under U.N. supervision in return for food, medicine, and other necessities. Many feel that only strict enforcement of the sanctions will force Hussein from office. And only then will the economy be able to improve.

Petroleum and Mining

In 1980, before the war with Iran, Iraq was the second-largest supplier of crude oil. Only Saudi Arabia produced more. Petroleum accounted for 95 percent of the foreign money that Iraq earned.

Opposite: **A damaged oil refinery**

Working in a refinery

Iranian military strikes knocked out key Iraqi oil terminals. Refineries, pipelines, pumping stations, and petrochemical plants were damaged. Then, in the Persian Gulf War of 1991, Allied forces' bombing again hurt the industry.

Iraq concentrated on trying to restore its production of crude petroleum. Petroleum is important to keep the country's transportation running and lights operating. Smugglers barter it for goods that are hard to obtain in Iraq. The sanctions, however, have cost Iraq millions in lost sales.

In addition to petroleum, Iraq has reserves of natural gas, sulfur, natural phosphates, salt, and gypsum. However, petroleum is the key to Iraq's recovery and ability to get foreign money.

Agriculture

Agriculture is now the most important sector of the Iraqi economy. Before the Persian Gulf War, Iraq imported about 70 percent of its food supplies at a cost of $1.1 billion. Now, a food-rationing system provides each person with 1,300 calories and six grams of protein daily. The unrest caused by the increase in prices and the collapse of the currency was met by tight government security. The rationing system at least prevents starvation but it is very hard on some Iraqis—especially city dwellers. A farming family can eat well, but in Baghdad, a family may be limited to rice, yogurt, and bread.

A woman with her food rations for two months

In 1958, land reform required a redistribution of property. Cooperatives and state farms were set up, with disappointing results. More private ownership was then allowed. Now state farms have been abolished and individuals are allowed to lease land at low rates.

Some farms have been successful; others have failed.

After the Persian Gulf War, production decreased. Upkeep of irrigation and drainage systems was difficult. Farmers were unable to get pesticides and fertilizers because of possible war-related use of the chemicals. Harvests have been poor.

Iraq grows a wide variety of crops. The most important are barley and wheat, but good rainfall is necessary for the best yields. Maize, sugar beet and cane, and melons are also cultivated. Egg and chicken production is important, too. Dates are the country's main cash crop.

As in ancient times, the water supply is of major importance. Given other economic conditions, Iraq could double the amount of cultivated land in the country. Dams and reservoirs provide some protection against flooding and permit the creation of hydroelectric power from water. Stagnant (standing) water is a problem because it adds to the salts in the soil.

Industry

Before 1970, there were few large industries other than petroleum. Around Baghdad, some large companies dealt with electricity, water supply, and building materials. Smaller industrial units were involved with date-packing, breweries, cigarettes, textiles, chemicals, furniture, shoes, jewelry, and metal-working.

After 1970, new industries developed, including iron and steel, sulfur and phosphate products, textiles, sugar refineries, and cement works. The most recent projects included pharmaceuticals, electrical goods, telephone cables, and plastics.

What Iraq Grows, Makes, and Mines

Agriculture (1995)

Wheat	1,320,000 metric tons
Barley	990,000 metric tons
Tomatoes	870,000 metric tons

Manufacturing *(in millions of Iranian dinar; 1990)*

Petroleum products	668
Nonmetal mineral products	152
Food	114

Mining

None

Electronics manufacturing is one growing industry in Iraq.

During the war with Iran, the nation's electrical power stations were bombed. Iraq later worked to improve and extend its electrical networks. In 1991, the U.N. forces effectively wiped out all electrically powered installations by bombing power plants. Industrial production dropped drastically. After the war, trade sanctions made it difficult to get spare parts and raw materials. Unemployment soared.

Iraq's experimental nuclear reactor was bombed by the Israeli air force in 1981. France, Saudi Arabia, Brazil, Portugal, Italy, and the former Soviet Union were reportedly involved in helping Iraq to establish a new reactor. Now, the U.N. is attempting to oversee the destruction of Iraq's potential for developing nuclear weapons.

An Iraqi airport damaged during the war

Communications and Transportation

In the 1981–85 Iraqi plan, communications and transportation received special attention. The 1980–88 war with Iran caused Iraq to concentrate on building a network of roads to help move troops. That conflict also destroyed transportation facilities—especially around the gulf port of Basra. Years of work will be needed to clean up the bombs and wreckage from the Shatt al-Arab waterway where fighting was heavy. In the Persian Gulf War, Iraq's civilian and military airports suffered heavy damage. Attempts are being made to restore the transportation systems with considerable success.

Communications also have been modernized. Many people rely on radio and television. In Iraq, the government operates these stations.

Finance and Trade

Iraq has few banks. The Central Bank of Iraq has the sole right to issue money, and there are two nationalized commercial banks. Three private commercial banks were founded

The government controls television programming.

recently. Four specialized banks service the areas of agriculture, industry, real estate, and loans to civil servants and
decorated veterans of the Iran–Iraq War. At present, many
people barter their services for things they need.

Today, the U.N. sanctions govern what can be purchased
from—or sold to—Iraq. Before the Persian Gulf War, Iraq
traded with Europe, the United States, Japan, and Turkey.
Trade with the Soviet Union was limited to military supplies.

The United Nations Security
Council voting on sanctions
against Iraq

Until the Iran–Iraq War, Iraq had not found it necessary to borrow from other countries although the other Arab countries and Europe had been willing to lend money to the government. Iraq was then seen as a block to Iran's expansion and terrorism. Now, Iraqi foreign debt has zoomed because of the country's responsibility for damage done to civilians and to other countries in the Persian Gulf War. Iraq is left with an estimated $200 billion owed to others.

Family and Tribe

Approximately 20 million people live in Iraq. This population is large enough to provide the labor that will be needed for industrial growth and to keep reinforcing an army. The nation's agriculture can support the increase that may be expected with better health care. However, a sizable population can be a problem if food is scarce.

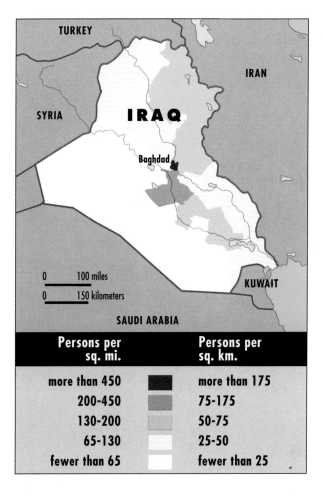

Iraq's Major Cities

Baghdad	4,478,000
Basra	1,500,000
Mosul	1,250,000

Ｍost of Iraq's people live in cities and towns. Many people from rural areas have moved to urban centers to seek better wages.

Who Are You?

Your family, your tribe, your religious group—in Iraq, these facts decide who you are. Your lifestyle depends on the group you come from. You are expected to help your family, and your family is expected to help you.

The three major groups are the Sunni Kurds, the Sunni Arabs, and the Shiite Arabs. While 62.5 percent of the people are Shiites, the leaders of the party in power since 1968 are mostly Sunnis. The Kurds live in the north, while the Shiites are concentrated in the south.

A very small population of Jews live in Iraq. Some Jewish people date their families to the Babylonian exile of the

Map labels: TURKEY, IRAN, SYRIA, IRAQ, Baghdad, KUWAIT, SAUDI ARABIA

0 — 100 miles
0 — 150 kilometers

Persons per sq. mi.		Persons per sq. km.
more than 450		more than 175
200-450		75-175
130-200		50-75
65-130		25-50
fewer than 65		fewer than 25

Who Lives in Iraq?

Arabs	80%
Kurds	15%
Other	5%

(including Marsh Arabs, Yezidis, Turkomans, Sabaeans, and Jazirah Bedouins)

Hello

In Iraq, you shake hands with a friend when you meet and when you part. You greet a good friend of the same sex with a kiss on both cheeks. Men and women shake hands. When you meet a small group for the first time, you are introduced individually to each person. First names are used as soon as you are introduced.

The family provides identity in Iraq.

Jews (586-516 B.C.). Recently, most of the Jews left Iraq because of Iraqi anger at the founding of the Jewish state of Israel.

A number of Christian communities are related to different denominations. They are descendants of people who did not convert to Islam when the religion was introduced. The Assyrians are Christian descendants of ancient Mesopotamians and speak Aramaic. Some of them now live in the United States and Canada.

Other minorities include the Yazidis of Kurdish background—who have a religion of their own—the Turkomans speaking a Turkish dialect, and a small number of Armenians.

Arabic Numbers

0	*sifir*
1	*wahid*
2	*ithneen*
3	*thalatha*
4	*arba'a*
5	*khamsa*
6	*sitta*
7	*sab'a*
8	*thimania*
9	*tis'a*
10	*ashra*
11	*hda'ash*
12	*thna'ash*

Pronunciation Key

Some of the sounds in Iraqi Arabic are unlike those that Americans and Canadians are accustomed to using. For example, g is a gargle-like sound; r is trilled; and x is said to be like a sound made in clearing your throat. You may be able to hear these sounds on a language audiotape in your library.

Opposite: **Arabic writing can be very ornate.**

What Language Do You Speak?

The official language of Iraq is Arabic. An estimate of languages spoken is: Arabic, 75 percent; Kurdish, 15 to 20 percent; Persian, 3 percent; and Turkish, 2 percent.

Although written Arabic is the same throughout the Arab world, there are many spoken dialects that often differ by country—including the dialect spoken in Iraq.

Written Arabic is read from right to left. There are three different forms of the language: classical (used in the Koran); modern everyday; and a fancier literary form. There are also different styles of writing—thicker characters for everyday use and thinner, more elaborate characters for special uses.

Iraqi Kurds speaks two Kurdish dialects, but they can understand other dialects. Kurdish is written with the Arabic alphabet.

Islam's Influence

Even before Islam came to Iraq, the religious life of
this land had an important influence on others. The
myths and ideas of the early Sumerians were carried
to other lands. Most famous is the Epic of Gilgamesh.
Many religions have swept through the land that is
now Iraq during its long history, but Islam is now the
state religion, with freedom of religion promised by
the constitution.

Teachings of Islam

ISLAM MEANS SUBMISSION TO THE WILL OF GOD (ALLAH IN Arabic). Islam, like Christianity and Judaism, focuses on one God. The faith of Islam is summed up in the shahada: "There is no God but God, and Muhammad is his Prophet." The Koran is the holy book that contains the inspired words of Muhammad given by God through the Angel Gabriel. The Muslims (followers of Islam) honor this book and believe it contains everything humans need for salvation.

The Muslims also believe that the Christian gospels, the first five books of the Old Testament, and the psalms are

Gilgamesh

Gilgamesh, a kind of god-man, meets an uncivilized hunter named Enkidu. After fighting, the two make friends and set out to see the world. Enkidu angers the gods and is struck down with a long disease from which he dies. Gilgamesh goes in search of eternal life. Along the way he meets a man who, on the advice of a god, built a boat and survived a flood that was supposed to wipe out all humans. Gilgamesh is said to have found eternal life in a plant growing at the bottom of the ocean. On his way home, when he is asleep, a snake steals the plant. Gilgamesh is left with the prospect of dying like ordinary humans.

A page from the Koran

inspired. However, they think the texts we have today are not as God gave them. Muslims recognize Adam, Noah, Abraham, Moses, and Jesus as great prophets, but for them Muhammad is the last and greatest prophet.

The Hadith contains traditions based on sayings and deeds of Muhammad. The Koran and the Hadith provide the basis for the code of behavior that governs Muslims. That code is called the Sunna. The two main groups of Muslims, the Sunnis and Shiites, have different Sunna.

A mosque and its minaret

Practices of Islam

Saying the shahada once, aloud, with understanding and belief is necessary to become a Muslim.

Praying five times a day while facing Mecca is required. Next to the mosques—buildings set aside for group prayer and worship—are minarets, or towers. From these minarets, a person (or more recently, a loudspeaker) calls the faithful to prayer at the required times.

Friday is the day when Muslims gather in their mosque to pray and to hear a sermon. The preachers, called imams, are teachers, not priests with religious authority to stand between the worshiper and God.

Fasting is required during the month of Ramadan. No food, drink, tobacco, or other worldly pleasure may be taken from dawn until sunset. Ramadan falls at different times in different years because it is determined by a calendar based on the moon. When it falls during the long, hot days of summer, fasting is not easy. Exceptions are made for the sick, the weak, soldiers, and travelers.

The Five Pillars of Islam
- The shahada emphasizing the oneness of God
- The duty to pray five times a day
- Fasting
- Giving to others
- Pilgrimage to Mecca

Muhammad
Muhammad, the founder of Islam, lived in what is now Saudi Arabia. He was born in Mecca in 570 and died in 632. He is buried in Medina.

Giving to the poor and to the mosques is a duty. Even with a state-provided welfare system, generosity to others is valued.

The pilgrimage to Mecca is expected of every Muslim who can afford to go. The Shiites also make pilgrimage to one of the great Shiite holy places in Iraq.

As with other religions, attention to these practices varies. For a while, Muslims who had been influenced by other cultures took a more relaxed view of these duties, and so did the poorer working classes. However, there has been a renewed interest in following these practices throughout the Arab world. Iraq took a liberal view of these five duties at the beginning of the revolutionary movement, but now the government seems to be taking a more orthodox stand.

An Iraqi's World

An Iraqi's world begins with the family, but it extends to an interest in the arts, sports, and politics. In some ways, it has been very much a man's world with the Arab's protection of women of the family. Yet, even in the past, women enjoyed a good deal of power within the home. In the marketplace, they have the example of Muhammad's wife, a shrewd businesswoman.

IRAQ IS ONE OF THE ARAB COUNTRIES that has encouraged women to get an education and to enter the job market. Saddam Hussein's wife worked as a schoolteacher. Many women hold professional positions. Still, the opportunities for a woman may depend on the values of her family and the part of the country in which she lives.

Sajida Khayrallah, the wife of Saddam Hussein

Women hold all sorts of professional positions in Iraq.

The long periods of war and life in a dictatorship have made Iraqis cautious and secretive. Recent food shortages have added to their hardship. Many former soldiers seen on the streets have lost limbs in the fighting.

The family provides a strong support and social system. Family ties reach beyond the father, mother, and children to include grandparents, aunts, uncles, and cousins. These strong bonds have been helpful to people who have suffered deprivation. On the other hand, many Iraqi families have lost the financial and emotional support of family members killed in the Iran–Iraq and the Persian Gulf wars.

A wedding is a special celebration in Iraq.

An Iraqi Wedding

According to one description of a traditional wedding, on the big day, the bride sits all day in her father's house in her white gown. Her hands and feet are decorated with red henna. She receives her female guests, who admire her clothing and her father's gifts. The gold jewelry she wears is important insurance for her in case her husband divorces her. The bride is not supposed to notice anything on her wedding day, so she stares straight ahead.

That evening, the wedding drums beat. Pipers play the music for the traditional dances. The bridegroom washes his face and hands. Then he is led by the Islamic teacher to the bride's house where the marriage contract is signed.

Honor and protection of one's family have always been important virtues in Iraq. One of the methods used by Saddam Hussein's security forces to force people to talk or cooperate is to hurt or kill a family member in their presence. Even children and young people have been tortured.

Much of an Iraqi's happiness in life comes from family celebrations. The birth of a son is a special joy because the son will stay with the family and carry on family traditions. A daughter will marry and move to her husband's family home.

Traditional families arrange marriages. Often, the mother decides whom her sons will marry. After all, the new daughter-in-law will move into the home of the son's mother. In rural areas, there may be no place for a woman to live except the house of her father, her husband, her brother, or her son. Today, however, there is more consultation with the young people involved.

A procession by boat for a marshland traditional wedding

Legally, a Muslim may have four wives, but this is rare because of the expense. Not only is the man expected to make a gift to his bride, he must also make sure she is treated as well as his other wives. It is unusual for a man to have even two wives because then there is the question of which wife is in

command—and of what. The status of a second wife is better than that of an unmarried woman.

A woman who lives in the city has more options, though she is still tied closely to her family. Baghdad boasts a large educated middle class.

Death in the family also is observed with ceremony. Burial is prompt and handled by the men of the family. There is a ritual period of mourning. Women visit a woman who has lost a family member.

Only men attend funerals.

Opposite:
(above) **The main gate of Babylon built during the reign of Nebuchadrezzar II, now in a museum**

(below) **The Monument to the Revolution in Baghdad**

Iraqi Arts

Iraq has had a rich cultural life. The ancient traditions in architecture, sculpture, painting, weaving and carpetmaking, and prose and poetry have been carried on in modern times. The ministry of culture and information works to preserve the past while encouraging artists of today.

In Baghdad, ancient monuments stand next to modern steel, glass, and concrete buildings. The government has encouraged modern art by sending students abroad to study; modern sculpture and painting are appreciated. Statues depicting Iraqi history are placed in public parks.

Museums in Iraq encourage artists by acquiring their works and by arranging exhibitions. The National Museum of Modern Art in Baghdad is important to artists for these reasons.

Few countries can boast of such rich archaeological treasures as Iraq. The Iraq Museum has halls arranged chronologically to cover these civilizations: pre-history, Sumerians, Akkadians, Baby-

Many children study ballet in Iraq.

lonians, Assyrians, Chaldeans, Seleucids, Parthians, Sassanians, and Abbasids. The museum also houses a fine library of books in many languages for visiting scholars.

In addition to traditional Arabic music and dancing, Baghdad is home to the Music and Ballet School and the National Symphony Orchestra. Theater and films are also supported.

Poets and prose writers are honored in Iraq. Arabic culture has a long tradition of fine poetry, and poetry festivals attract many people. Many poems written today have a political theme. Iraqi poets, including a woman, Nazik al-Malaikah, are among the pioneers of free verse in Arabic.

All mass media are under government control. The major daily newspapers are published in Arabic, along with a variety of periodicals. Radio broadcasts are presented in several languages, and the country has at least twenty-four television stations.

Even newspapers are under government control.

Writers and artists have suffered during the recent wars and their aftermath. The embargoes have prevented books and supplies reaching them. The professional classes have found the economic hardships very difficult. Who will trade

A Night on the Town

The 1,000-seat National Theater in Baghdad was one of the most modern and best equipped in the Arab world when it was built. Its revolving stage is 49 feet (15 meters) in diameter and its two halls for movie projection provide plenty of space for plays, concerts, and films.

food for a poem? Most people would rather trade for a car repair. Many intellectuals have had to sell their books to live.

The difficult economic period has also affected educational opportunities. Without books, Iraqis are falling behind in scientific subjects. In 1997, it was reported that a notebook for an elementary-school student cost 8 percent of the average monthly salary of a civil servant.

Opposite: **Soccer is a popular Iraqi sport.**

Iraqi Sports and Games

Iraqis enjoy soccer, horse racing, backgammon, and chess. Basketball, volleyball, weightlifting, and boxing also are popular. At one point, a number of sports clubs were listed for Baghdad including a hunt club, a horsemanship club, and a chess club. There are three stadiums in Baghdad.

Uday Hussein, Saddam's son, heads the Iraq Football Federation and the Iraqi Olympic Committee.

A Defection

On July 31, 1996, Raed Ahmed, the Iraqi weightlifter who carried his country's flag at the opening ceremonies of the Olympics, defected. Asking for political asylum, he stated that he was persecuted in Iraq for being a Shiite Muslim. Ahmed reported that the U.S. Immigration and Naturalization Service granted him asylum.

An Iraqi's World **119**

An Iraqi Youngster's Day

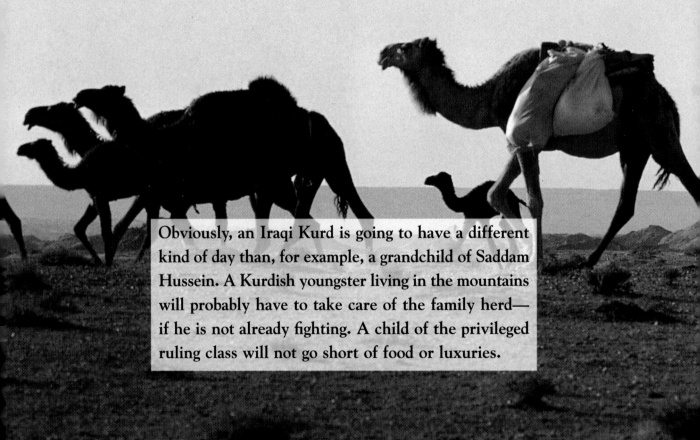

Obviously, an Iraqi Kurd is going to have a different kind of day than, for example, a grandchild of Saddam Hussein. A Kurdish youngster living in the mountains will probably have to take care of the family herd— if he is not already fighting. A child of the privileged ruling class will not go short of food or luxuries.

THE LIFE OF A SUNNI ARAB LIVING IN the desert is different from that of a Shiite Arab living in the marshes. The desert Arab knows how to ride horses and camels—and probably knows how to drive trucks. The Marsh Arab, if Saddam Hussein has not drained off the water around the youngster's home, knows how to get around by boat, how to use reeds as building materials, and how to hunt wild pigs.

What is life like for the average youngster in Baghdad? Let's imagine a year when food is plentiful and the family has no war casualties. Let's call him Ali and imagine he has a younger sister named Laila.

Some Iraqi children can get around by boat.

What Would a Day Be Like for Ali?

At dawn, the first call to prayer is heard from the minarets. Ali rises, goes through a ritual of washing. Then from a standing position, Ali bows and prostrates himself, touching his forehead to the ground while silently reciting a quotation from

A typical Iraqi breakfast

the Koran. He will pray also at noon, in late afternoon, at sunset, and after sunset. The prayers may be performed anywhere though there may be special merit in going to the mosque. Friday is the day for congregational prayers in the mosque.

At breakfast, around 7 A.M., Ali might have pita bread (a circular puffy bread), cheese with dibis (date syrup), butter, eggs, and milk. If it is a school day, Ali and his sister will go to class. All children from age six to twelve are required to attend school. Their parents do not have to pay for their education. Secondary education begins at age twelve in two series of three years each. Boys are more likely to continue their

education than girls are. Both Ali and Laila can expect to go to university if they wish, and if they are good students.

Lunch could be a stew of lamb, vegetables, tomatoes, fresh lemon, and garlic with rice. Salad, bread, and fruit are often served with the main dish. After school, Ali might kick around a soccer ball with some of his friends.

Laila and her mother might visit a friend of her mother's who also has daughters, and they might talk about the latest fashions and entertainment. In the evening when it is cool, they may visit a souk, one of the busy bazaars with many small shops.

Soccer is fun anywhere in the world.

Shopping in one of Iraq's souks

At tea time, 5 or 6 P.M., the youngsters might enjoy a snack of bread and cheese or watermelon with cheese. Then, if their parents are having guests for dinner, Ali and Laila will eat by themselves. For the guests, there may be special dishes, such as a shish kebab (skewers with ground lamb mixed with parsley and onion) and rice. Masgouf, a fish from the Tigris River, is another Iraqi delicacy. It is split down the middle, opened, and grilled outdoors on a stick and is served with lime chutney or Indian curries.

All the dishes may be placed in the center of the table, and the diners then take small helpings on their own plates. Westerners must be careful not to dip into the food with their left hands. In desert countries, the left hand is used for toilet functions and is considered unclean. After the guests leave the table, fruit will be served.

Ali and Laila might look forward to some of the Muslim holidays when it is customary for friends of the family to give money or small gifts to children.

Iraq's Holidays

New Year's Day	January 1
Army Day	January 6
Fourteenth Ramadan Revolution Day	February 8
Declaration of the Republic	July 14
Peaceful Revolution Day	July 17

Opposite: **Fish is often grilled outdoors.**

What Do Ali and Laila Wear?

Because these youngsters live in Baghdad, they may wear Western clothes. However, with Iraq's increasing attention to Islamic customs, Laila will have to dress modestly and perhaps wear a head covering. Many Arab women wear the traditional abaya, a long black cloak that covers their clothes. A Kurdish girl, also a Muslim, may wear clothes of bright colors and a simple head scarf.

An Arab man in desert dress wears a head scarf that is held on with two circles of black rope. The rope was originally used to hobble a camel's legs so that it would not run away.

A woman in a traditional abaya

A man in desert dress

What Do Ali and Laila Think About Most?

Ali can expect to serve in the military forces when he is seventeen. His service will last eighteen months to two years, but it can be extended in time of war. Surely, Ali must wonder what his fate will be if there is another war.

Women may serve in the Iraqi military.

The big change in Laila's life will come when she marries and joins another family. How will she get along with her mother-in-law and the rest of the family? Will she have a son that will give her special status? Will she decide to follow a career and have more independence with money of her own to spend? These questions are not always decided by girls like Laila. Much depends on the wealth, education, and traditions of her family.

What Is the Heritage of Ali and Laila?

Ali and Laila live in a country whose people have contributed much to our civilization—writing, counting, the wheel, a calendar, agriculture, the study of nature.

Let us hope that Ali and Laila will one day live in a country that is free of the threats that now surround them. Ali and

Laila will have to figure out a way to cooperate with others in their country—the Kurds and the Shiites. Then they will be able to take advantage of the rich natural resources with which Iraq is blessed.

The future of Iraq is in the hands of the young.

Timeline

Iraqi History

Use of copper begins in Mesopotamia	5000 B.C.
Writing begins in Sumer; wheeled vehicles in use	3300
Writing in Assyria	2400
Rule of Sargon I, first known empire	2350
Supremacy of Ur in lower Mesopotamia	2100 – 2000
Rule of Hammurabi in Babylonia	1750
Fall of the Dynasty of Hammurabi	1600
Beginning of a century of Assyrian conquest	744
Assyria destroys the kingdom of Israel	722
Sargon II takes Babylon	710
Persians destroy Nineveh	612
Alexander the Great captures Babylon	331
Alexander the Great dies in Babylon	323
Birth of Muhammad in Mecca	c. 570 A.D.
Arabs conquer Iraq	637
Umayyads move Caliphate of Islam to Baghdad	661
Shiite revolt in Iraq	685 – 686
Mansur founds Baghdad as new capital	762 – 763

World History

2500 B.C.	Egyptians build the Pyramids and Sphinx in Giza.
563 B.C.	Buddha is born in India.
A.D. 313	The Roman emperor Constantine recognizes Christianity.
610	The prophet Muhammad begins preaching a new religion called Islam.

	Iraqi History		World History

Iraqi History

Monguls sack Baghdad	1258
Tamerlane ravages Iraq	1379–1401
Ottomans seize Iraq	1534
Ottoman Empire enters World War I on the side of the Central Powers (Germany)	1914
Collapse of Ottoman Empire, end of World War I	1916
League of Nations gives Britain a mandate over Iraq	1920
Faisal I becomes King of Iraq	1921
Iraq granted full independence; admitted to the League of Nations	1932
Formation of the Arab League	1945
First Arab–Israeli War	1948–1949
Military revolt topples monarchy	1958
Baath Party takes control of Iraq	1968
Saddam Hussein becomes President	1979
Iran–Iraq War	1980–1988
Iraq invades Kuwait	1990
Persian Gulf War	1991

World History

1054	The Eastern (Orthodox) and Western (Roman) Churches break apart.
1066	William the Conqueror defeats the English in the Battle of Hastings.
1095	Pope Urban II proclaims the First Crusade.
1215	King John seals the Magna Carta.
1300s	The Renaissance begins in Italy.
1347	The Black Death sweeps through Europe.
1453	Ottoman Turks capture Constantinople, conquering the Byzantine Empire.
1492	Columbus arrives in North America.
1500s	The Reformation leads to the birth of Protestantism.
1776	The Declaration of Independence is signed.
1789	The French Revolution begins.
1865	The American Civil War ends.
1914	World War I breaks out.
1917	The Bolshevik Revolution brings Communism to Russia.
1929	Worldwide economic depression begins.
1939	World War II begins, following the German invasion of Poland.
1957	The Vietnam War starts.
1989	The Berlin Wall is torn down, as Communism crumbles in Eastern Europe.
1996	Bill Clinton re-elected U.S. president.

Fast Facts

Official name: Republic of Iraq (Al-Jumhuriyah al-Iraqiyah)

Capital: Baghdad

Official language: Arabic, spoken by about 75% of Iraq's people

Official religion:	Islam
National anthem:	Salute of the Republic (Al-Salaam al-Jumhuri)
Government:	Unitary multiparty republic with one legislative house (National Assembly of 250).
Area:	167,925 sq mi (434,924 sq km)
Bordering countries:	Turkey, Syria, Jordan, Saudi Arabia, Kuwait, and Iran.

Average temperatures:	in summer	in winter
	120°F (49°C)	50°F (10°C)

National population:
(1995 est.) 20,413,000

Population of major
cities in Iraq:
(1995 est.)

Baghdad (urban total)	4,478,000
Basra	1,500,000
Mosul	1,250,000

Famous landmarks: The ancient civilizations that once flourished in Mesopotamia have left Iraq dotted with ancient ruins. Among them are Ashur (or Assur), Nineveh, Babylon, Nimrud, Hatra, and Ur of the Chaldees. These sites can be visited but many of their splen-

did artifacts can be seen at the Iraqi Museum in Baghdad and the Mosul Museum. Also in Baghdad, located in restored 13th and 14th century buildings, are the Abbasid Palace Museum and the Museum of Arab Antiquities.

Industry: Oil is by far the largest export of Iraq. United Nations sanctions currently forbid export of Iraqi oil supplies. Important cash crops include dates, wheat, barley, and cotton. Food processing, textiles, and leather goods are major industries in Iraq. There are few mineral deposits currently being exploited in Iraq with the exception of oil.

Currency: 1 Iraqi dinar (ID) = 1,000 fils; approximate valuation in 1997: 1 U.S.$ = 2,600 ID

Weights and measures: Imperial system

Literacy: Virtually 100%

Arabic words and phrases:

Dijlah	term for the Tigris
Al-Furatan	term for the Euphrates
hajj	a pilgrimage to Mecca
hejira	the pilgrimage made by Muhammad from Mecca to Medina
shamal	the summer northwesterly wind that blows in Iraq
sharqi	the strong southeasterly wind that blows during Iraq's winter
Shari'a	the Islamic law code
Vilayat	term referring to the provinces of the Ottoman Empire; Iraq comprised the Ottoman Vilayats of Mosul, Baghdad, and Basra

To Find Out More

Ancient History

▶ Foster, Leila Merrell. *The Sumerians.* New York: Franklin Watts, 1990.

▶ Editors of Time-Life Books. *Sumer: Cities of Eden.* Alexandria, VA: Time-Life Books, 1993.

▶ Editors of Time-Life Books. *Mesopotamia: The Mighty Kings.* Alexandria, VA: Time-Life Books, 1995.

▶ Glubok, Shirley, ed. *Discovering the Royal Tombs at Ur.* London: The Macmillan Company, 1969.

Modern History

▶ Foster, Leila Merrell. *The Story of the Persian Gulf War.* Chicago: Childrens Press, 1991.

▶ King, John. *Kurds.* New York: Thomson Learning, 1993.

▶ Pimlott, John. *Middle East: A Background to the Conflicts.* New York: Gloucester Press, 1991.

▶ Steins, Richard. *The Mideast after the Gulf War.* Brookfield, CT: Millbrook Press, 1992.

▶ Stefoff, Rebecca. *Saddam Hussein: Absolute Ruler of Iraq.* Brookfield, CT: Millbrook Press, 1995.

Nonfiction

▶ Dudley, William, and Stacey L. Tipp, eds. *Current Controversies: Iraq.* San Diego, CA: Greenhaven Press, 1991.

▶ Kent, Zachary. *The Persian Gulf War: "The Mother of All Battles."* Springfield, NJ: Enslow Publishers, 1994.

▶ Stefoff, Rebecca. *Saddam Hussein: Absolute Ruler of Iraq.* Brookfield, CT: Millbrook Press, 1995.

Fiction

▶ Ayoub, Abderrahman, Jamila Binous, Abderrazak Gragueb, Ali Mtimet, and Hedi Slim. *Umm Al Madayan: An Islamic City Through the Ages.* Boston: Houghton Mifflin, 1994.

▶ Lang, Edward, ed. *Arabian Nights.* New York: Longmans, Green & Co., 1946.

Websites

▶ **ArabNet—Iraq**
http://www.arab.net/iraq/ iraq_contents.html
Complete informational site on Iraq, its history, its culture, and its people.

▶ **Iraq Foundation**
http://www.iraqfoundation.org/
The Iraq Foundation works for democracy and human rights in Iraq.

▶ **The Iraqi National Congress**
http://www.inc.org.uk/
Website for the opposition party to Saddam Hussein's rule in Iraq.

▶ **Iraq—A Country Study**
http://lcweb2.loc.gov/frd/cs/iqtoc.html
Well-laid out site maintained by the Library of Congress. The site contains a wide range of historical and cultural information on Iraq.

Organizations and Embassies

Iraqi Embassy
Iraqi Interests Section
c/o Embassy of Algeria
1801 P. Street, NW
Washington, DC 20036
202-483-7500

Index

Meet the Author

LEILA MERRELL FOSTER has traveled extensively in the Middle East. She visited Iraq in 1962 on a trip around the world with her father. It was the only country from which she could not get a visa to enter before she left her home in the United States. She and her dad had to go to the Iraqi embassy in Iran and ask to visit Iraq. Fortunately, they were given permission to enter the country, so she was able to see Baghdad, Babylon, and Ctesiphon and visit the fine museum in the capital.

In writing this book, she read about the ancient and modern history and also followed the television and newspaper accounts of the latest skirmishes with Saddam Hussein. She went to the Evanston Public Library and the Northwestern University Library. Then she checked out the Internet and discovered that the CIA has a *World Fact Book* for different countries. On the MIT website, she found pictures of Iraq. A number of museums such as the Oriental Institute at the

University of Chicago have pictures on the web of ancient items in their collections.

She has written other books about the region: *The Sumerians*, *The Story of the Persian Gulf War*, *Saudi Arabia*, *Lebanon*, and *Jordan*. Also, she is a lawyer, a United Methodist minister, and a clinical psychologist. Travel and photography are her favorite hobbies. Once she has visited a country, she enjoys keeping up on the news from there.

Photo Credits

Photographs ©:

AKG London: 35;

Ancient Art & Architecture Collection: 31 top (R. Sheridan), 60;

AP/Wide World Photos: 65 top;

Archive Photos: 66 top;

Art Resource: 36 (Giraudon), 30, 48 top, 62, 115 top (Erich Lessing), 39 bottom, 41 bottom, 50 bottom, 54, 56 (Scala);

Black Star: 123 bottom (Peter Turnley), 116 (David Turnley/Corbis), 76, 107 bottom, 126 (David Turnley/Detroit Free Press), 100 (Peter Turnley/Newsweek);

Christina Dameyer: 125 left;

Comstock: 34 (George Gerster), 17 bottom, 24;

e.t. archive: 31 bottom, 43 top, 61;

Gamma-Liaison: 87 top (Noel Quidu), 131 top (Claude Salhani), 87 bottom, 93 (Anthony Suau), 91 bottom (L. Van Der Stockt), 7 center, 67 top, 119;

Globe Photos: 75, 127 (Arnaud Fevrier);

The Image Works: 107 top (Bob Strong), cover, back cover, 6 (Topham);

Impact Visuals: 11 top (Henrik Saxgren);

Magnum Photos: 74 (Abbas), 12 (Bruno Barbey), 111 bottom (Steve McCurry);

National Geographic Image Collection: 2, 84, 85, 120, 130 (Lynn Abercrombie), 23, 72, 73 (Steve McCurry);

Nik Wheeler: 8, 13, 14, 16 bottom, 17 top, 18, 19, 90, 98, 103, 110, 112, 113, 114, 118, 121, 122, 123 top, 124, 125 right, 133;

North Wind Picture Archives: 27 top right, 48 bottom, 50 top;

Peter Arnold Inc.: 86, cover spine, 132 bottom (Ingeborg Lippman);

Photo Researchers: 108, 109, 132 top (Mehmet Biber), 28 bottom (Jose Luis G. Grande), 27 bottom (Tom McHugh), 83 (Guy Trouvenin), 29 (David Weintraur);

Photofest: 59;

Photri: 20 top, 44;

Reuters/Corbis-Bettmann: 69, 71, 89, 91 top, 95, 96, 97, 101, 117;

Stern: 11 bottom (Perry Kretz);

Superstock, Inc.: 16 top, 22 bottom, 115 bottom, 131 bottom;

Sygma: 80 (Mathieson), 94 (Orban), 9 bottom (J. Pavlovsky), 9 top (Joseph Tual), 88;

UPI/Corbis-Bettmann: 7 bottom, 37 top, 38, 39 top, 40, 41 top, 42, 43 bottom, 45, 47, 51, 52, 53, 63, 64, 65 center, 65 bottom, 66 bottom, 67 bottom, 68, 70, 78, 79, 104, 105, 106, 111 top;

Valan Photos: 7 top, 20 bottom, 22 top, 28 top (Christine Osborne);

Viesti Associates, Inc.: 26, 27 top left, 37 bottom (J. Baptiste).

Maps by Joe LeMonnier.